40 Unamuno: Niebla

Critical Guides to Spanish Texts

EDITED BY JOHN VAREY, ALAN DEYERMOND, & CATHERINE DAVIES

UNAMUNO

NIEBLA

Paul R. Olson

Professor of Spanish
The Johns Hopkins University

Grant & Cutler Ltd
1996

© Grant & Cutler Ltd 1996

ISBN 0 7293 0177 X

First edition 1984
Reprinted, with a revised bibliography 1996

DEPÓSITO LEGAL: V. 4.935 - 1995

Printed in Spain by
Gráficas Soler, S.A., Valencia
for
GRANT & CUTLER LTD
55–57 GREAT MARLBOROUGH STREET, LONDON W1V 2AY

Contents

Preface to Second Printing

Although no interpretation of *Niebla* can ever be complete, I believe there is nothing in this Guide's interpretation which requires basic change. It would be well, however, to amend my comment in note 52 concerning textual variants in Augusto's final words to Víctor in chapter xvii. I there observed that the variant which gives the passage its strongest meaning is that of *6*, '[...] me estás inventando [...]', although the first edition (*1*) and those based on it (*8*, *37*) have '[...] me están inventando [...]'. I added that *6* gives no justification for this departure from previous editions, but it should have been added that the reading is, in fact, implicitly justified by *6*'s use of the third edition (also listed in *1*), which Unamuno was able to revise himself (in contrast to the second edition, of 1928, which he had never seen). This reading is also found in *36* and *38*.

Prefatory note

References to the text of *Niebla* are to the edition by Manuel García Blanco, in *Obras completas* (Madrid: Escelicer, 1967), II, pp.541-682. Chapters are indicated by lower-case roman numerals: (vii), and where necessary this is followed by a page number. Other works by Unamuno are also cited in this edition of *Obras completas*, with volume number in roman capitals followed by a page number: (VIII, 715).

Italic numerals in parentheses refer to the Bibliographical Note, and are where necessary followed by a page number: (*17*, p.74).

1. Introduction: 'Niebla' and the novels of Unamuno

Unamuno's novels extend over a period of thirty-four years of almost continuous creative effort, from *Paz en la guerra* (1897) to *San Manuel Bueno, mártir* (1931). The central place of *Niebla* (1914) in this sequence aptly symbolizes its central importance in Unamuno's fiction, in the sense that it is highly typical of his thought and artistry, and at the same time the most original of his novels.[1] In this chapter I seek to place it — thematically and in terms of technique — within the general canon of Unamuno's works. By comparing and contrasting it with the other novels I hope to give a broad understanding of its significance, which subsequent chapters of this study will make more precise.

When one begins, however, to compare this work to the rest of the novels, a question immediately arises as to which of Unamuno's works actually belong to that genre, and this in turn implies a question about his own conception of the novel. It is well known that he profoundly disliked the establishment of any rigid categories, whether of human beings through application of partisan or sectarian labels, or of works of literature in the conventional names of modes and genres. A passage in the prologue to *Niebla*, presumably written by one of the novel's characters, Víctor Goti, is most revealing in this respect:

> Don Miguel tiene la preocupación del bufo trágico y me
> ha dicho más de una vez que no quisiera morirse sin haber
> escrito una bufonada trágica o una tragedia bufa, pero no
> en que lo bufo o grotesco y lo trágico estén mezclados o

[1] A good measure of the breadth of the recognition *Niebla* has received is to be found in the number of its translations. The bibliography in the latest *Obras completas* (II, 61-86) lists eleven, to which may be added a second English translation by Anthony Kerrigan (*10*), surpassing by far any of the other full-length novels and by at least three the briefer *novelas ejemplares*. Other measures of its critical reception could be found in the number of studies devoted exclusively to it in comparison with those on other individual works.

yuxtapuestos, sino fundidos y confundidos en uno. Y como yo le hiciese observar que eso no es sino el más desenfrenado romanticismo, me contestó: 'No lo niego, pero con poner motes a las cosas no se resuelve nada. A pesar de mis más de veinte años de profesar la enseñanza de los clásicos, el clasicismo que se opone al romanticismo no me ha entrado. Dicen que lo helénico es distinguir, definir, separar; pues lo mío es indefinir, confundir.' (Prólogo, 545)

This professed tendency to *indefinir* suggests, of course, that any attempt to give a rigorous definition of Unamuno's conception of the novel will necessarily be highly problematic, but some idea of the kinds of text he regarded as constituting the canon of novels in his own work may be had by referring to the 'Historia de *Niebla*' which appeared as a prologue to the third edition of the novel in 1935. The list there begins with *Paz en la guerra*, followed by *Amor y pedagogía* (1902), the *Vida de Don Quijote y Sancho* (1905), and the short stories of *El espejo de la muerte* (1913). For the period following publication of *Niebla* he lists *Abel Sánchez* (1917), *La tía Tula* (1921), *Cómo se hace una novela* (1927), and *San Manuel Bueno, mártir, y tres historias más* (1933, although the first of these narratives had appeared in 1931).

In a number of ways the list is remarkably arbitrary, both in its inclusions and in its omissions. The *Vida de Don Quijote y Sancho*, for example, is essentially a commentary on Cervantes's version of the adventures of his two characters, and although it is not a literal re-creation of the Cervantine text, in the manner of Borges's Pierre Menard, neither is it an entirely original fictional narrative. The various editions of Unamuno's *Obras completas* include it in volumes consisting principally of essays.[2] Equally surprising may be his inclusion of *Cómo se hace una novela*, which is not so much a novel as a discussion of the novel Unamuno says he would write about his exile in Paris if he

---

[2] See, for example, *4*: III, 49-256. It is grouped with the novels, however, in *Miguel de Unamuno: Novela*, ed. Eugenio de Bustos Tovar (Madrid: Noguer), 1976, pp.597-894.

actually were to write one. In addition to a sketchy outline of that hypothetical narrative the work contains an account of the circumstances of his exile, a great deal of political commentary, and a series of reflections on his readings at the time, all of which interrupt and delay the narrative to such an extent that it recedes into the background of the author's concern throughout much of the text. The latest edition of the *Obras completas* includes it in a volume of autobiography and memoirs.[3]

If the inclusion of such works in Unamuno's list is surprising, one might almost say as much for the presence there of *El espejo de la muerte*, which is a collection of brief narratives, none of which is longer than five pages. Like the novel they are, of course, works of prose fiction, but the difference in length is not merely a superficial one in the distinction critics normally make between the novel and the short story, since it is assumed that a certain length is essential for the kind of development of character and plot one expects in the novel. Unamuno has nevertheless preferred to call the stories in this collection *novelas cortas* rather than *cuentos*, and one can scarcely debate his right to do so. Early uses in Spanish of the word *novela* serve, after all, to designate relatively short narratives, as in the case of Cervantes's *Novelas ejemplares* — modeled on the Italian *novella* — which specifically contrast with the lengthy *Historia verdadera* of Don Quijote. Yet given the Cervantine example, it is all the more surprising that the 'Historia de *Niebla*' does not also include the *Tres novelas ejemplares y un prólogo* of 1920, in which Unamuno had said that the prologue itself was also a novel, or the many *relatos novelescos* published in periodicals between 1886 and 1920.[4]

Considering, then, with what freedom Unamuno used the term *novela* in the 'Historia de *Niebla*', it appears that he could have applied it just as well to the book he published in 1924 under the title *Teresa*, in which a lengthy 'Presentación' is actually a short novel telling of the love of a young poet for the

[3] VIII, 709-69. See also my edition of this work (Madrid: Labor, 1977), which restores passages omitted in even the most recent *Obras completas* and corrects numerous errors from the Buenos Aires edition of 1927.

[4] These *relatos* were first published posthumously in *De esto y aquello* (Buenos Aires: Sudamericana, 1951).

Teresa of the title. The main body of the book consists, however, of works attributed to this fictional poet, and it is clear that Unamuno himself, like the majority of his readers, critics, and editors, regarded his work in verse as substantially distinct from all genres of prose.[5] Among these, however, Unamuno's tendency to *indefinir* is very marked, and in the 'Historia de *Niebla*' it is clear that the story is assimilated in Unamuno's terminology to the novel, in the sense that it is the term *novela* which is given to both. In terms of his actual narrative practice, however, it might be said that Unamuno tended to assimilate the novel to the story, the *novela* to the *novella*. The inclusion of the many interpolated tales in *Niebla* and the episodic character of many of the other novels suggest the theory that the short story or character sketch was, in fact, the basic form in which Unamuno conceived his works of narrative fiction, and that the longer texts are essentially expansions or combinations of such forms.[6]

In either case the application of the name *novela* to all forms of narrative prose, whether long or short, does not seem too difficult to accept, but assimilation to the novel of more essayistic works is more problematic. One might be tempted to explain it simply as another example of Unamuno's well-known fondness for paradox, or by regarding it as an arbitrary whim. Without denying, however, that paradox and arbitrary exercise of will are present in the 'Historia de *Niebla*', it may be possible to see an explanation for this particular paradox in a passage from *Cómo se hace una novela* which discusses historical writing as a process of creation and self-creation entirely analogous to that found in the writing of fiction. As projections of the novelist's or the historian's self, literary characters — *entes de ficción*, as they are called in *Niebla* — and historical characters appearing in books of history are of precisely the same order of

---

[5] The text of *Teresa* is to be found in *4*, VI, 551-667. The one critic of Unamuno's work who devotes a study to *Teresa* as a novel is Ricardo Gullón (*19*, 218-45). Gullón's argument is so convincing that the obvious differences between prose and verse forms are shown to be no inherent obstacle to discussion of the work as a novel.

[6] There is good reason for regarding *Paz en la guerra* as an expansion of the stories 'Solitaña' (1889), 'San Miguel de Basauri' (1892), and at least one other story, mentioned in the essay 'A lo que salga' (I, 1194-1204) but never published.

reality:

> He dicho que nosotros, los autores, los poetas, nos ponemos, nos creamos, en todos los personajes poéticos que creamos, hasta cuando hacemos historia, cuando poetizamos, cuando creamos personas de que pensamos que existen en carne y hueso fuera de nosotros. ¿Es que mi Alfonso XIII de Borbón y Habsburgo-Lorena, mi Primo de Rivera, mi Martínez Anido, mi Conde de Romanones, no son otras tantas creaciones mías, partes de mí, tan mías como mi Augusto Pérez, mi Pachico Zabalbide, mi Alejandro Gómez y todas las demás criaturas de mis novelas? Todos los que vivimos principalmente de la lectura y en la lectura, no podemos separar de los personajes poéticos o novelescos a los históricos. Don Quijote es para nosotros tan real y efectivo como Cervantes o más bien éste tanto como aquél. Todo es para nosotros libro, lectura; podemos hablar del Libro de la Historia, del Libro de la Naturaleza, del Libro del Universo. Somos bíblicos. Y podemos decir que en el principio fue el Libro. (VIII, 732)

If for men of letters all of life is *lectura*, this is chiefly because for them reality itself is a great book, a secular scripture which is the basis of every such *lectura*, and once King Alfonso XIII is embodied in a text as he is in the political commentary of *Cómo se hace una novela*, he is of exactly the same order of being as the protagonist of *Niebla*, just as that protagonist has the same degree of reality as the author who appears in the novel conversing with him. This is to say, as well, that the author, Unamuno, is viewed as having the same degree of fictionality as his character, Augusto Pérez, or that the reality of both of them is equally problematic; yet both of them share with the Alfonso XIII of Unamuno's political commentary the reality — however minimal and however problematic — of *lectura* and *escritura*, of existence founded in textuality.

In the final analysis, then, it can be said concerning Unamuno's conception of the novel and of literary genres that it was, indeed, arbitrary, but this was largely because he regarded all definitions of genre as arbitrary and all genres of prose as open forms, to which no rigorous definition can be given. Equally as arbitrary as any definitions, he obviously believed, are the names of things to which they are applied, and in this attitude he seems both to echo the nominalist tradition continuous in Western thought at least since the time of Plato's *Cratylus*, and to anticipate Saussure's concept of the linguistic sign.[7] I therefore suggest that it was this sense of the arbitrary nature of all names that made Unamuno feel he could not only apply the name *novela* to virtually any literary work he chose but could also invent a new name — *nivola*, for example — for works conventionally known as novels.

Despite his reluctance to establish conventional generic distinctions among his prose works, he has, nevertheless, made one basic distinction which has proved useful to his critics who seek to enhance understanding of his work by identifying and analyzing its basic types. This is the distinction he made a decade before the publication of *Niebla*, between the work of what he called an *escritor ovíparo*, who does research into the historical background of his novel, writes preliminary sketches of his characters, and carefully plans the structure of his entire work, and that of the *escritor vivíparo*, who writes *a lo que salga*, without previous conscious preparation, in a burst of spontaneous creativity.[8] It is to the question of *Niebla*'s place within such typologies, that of Unamuno and those of his critics, that we must now turn.

The earliest major study of this kind is an article by Leon

---

[7] See Ferdinand de Saussure, *Course in General Linguistics*, ed. Charles Bally and Albert Sechehaye, trans. Wade Baskin (New York: The Philosophical Library), 1959, pp.65-70. In the Platonic dialogue Cratylus is actually the exponent of a conception of the linguistic sign as natural or non-arbitrary. His opponent in the debate, Hermogenes, holds the view that the names of things are established by arbitrary convention. What I call the nominalist tradition is not strictly speaking a linguistic theory, since it refers to a debate between those who held the *realist* theory that universals are real entities (a profoundly idealist concept, despite the name) and the *nominalists* who held that they have no other reality than that of the common name given to them. I trust the relation between such a theory and Saussure's conception (as well as that of Hermogenes) is nevertheless clear.

[8] See the essays, 'De vuelta' (VIII, 206-07; April 1902), 'Escritor ovíparo' (VIII, 208-10; April, 1902), and 'A lo que salga' (I, 1194-1204; September, 1904).

Livingstone, published some five years after Unamuno's death, in which the critic proposed a two-way division among the novels, one type of which would consist of *Paz en la guerra*, with the other type consisting of all the rest (*29*). In its historical theme, abundant description, lengthy plot development, and contemplative tone, *Paz en la guerra* is very strikingly different from all the other novels, but Livingstone's principal basis for the distinction is Unamuno's own theory of the two radically different kinds of writers. Since Unamuno cites his first novel as a major example of works created in the manner of the *escritor ovíparo*, Livingstone's divisions have the virtue of corresponding to the novelist's own theory of the modes of composition, but his application of the term *nivola* to all of the other novels has seemed questionable to other critics.

Thus, in the study by Geoffrey Ribbans on *Amor y pedagogía* and *Niebla* in the development of Unamuno's novelistic art, we find complete acceptance of Livingstone's argument that *Paz en la guerra* ought to be seen as occupying a unique position among the novels, but Ribbans holds that only the first two novels which followed it ought to be regarded as true *nivolas*, and that the later works might more appropriately be referred to as skeleton-novels or novels of passion (*24*, p.107). His arguments in favor of this three-part division are, I believe, entirely convincing. He points out numerous similarities between the principal characters — and even some secondary ones — in the two novels as evidence that *Amor y pedagogía* can very nearly be regarded as a first draft of *Niebla*. In both works we find that the characters are essentially caricatures of human foibles, that they have names somehow symbolic of their condition, and that the structure of relations among them is essentially the same in both works. The central character in both novels is faced with a basic human problem of self-affirmation and autonomy, and in both the failure to resolve that problem leads to suicide.

In both works this problem is presented as being analogous to that of bringing into existence a literary work — and literary characters — out of the nothingness of the empty page, and we may therefore say that they are to a considerable extent meta-novels, that is, novels about the creation and the mode of being of literary entities at the same time that they are about the creation and mode of being of human entities.[9]

In Chapter 5 of this study I shall discuss in greater detail what I believe are the essential characteristics of the *nivola*, both in theory and in terms of the practice actually followed in *Niebla*. At this point, however, I must make a few observations about a third category of novels discernible in Unamuno's work, in addition to those represented by *Paz en la guerra* and the *nivolas*.

Ribbans's suggested use of the name skeleton-novel for the kind of works produced after *Niebla* is prompted by Unamuno's saying in the Prologue to the second edition of *Paz en la guerra* (1923) that after publishing his first novel he began to write 'novelas fuera de lugar y tiempo determinados, en esqueleto, a modo de dramas íntimos' (91). It appears from this statement that Unamuno's category of *novelas en esqueleto* would include the *nivolas*, but that would not prevent critics' use of such a phrase in a more restricted sense if they chose. Yet I believe it preferable for a number of reasons to use the alternate suggestion made by Ribbans for designating the third group of novels, that is, as novels of passion. The subtitle of *Abel Sánchez*, which is *Una historia de pasión*, makes the use of the term for the entire group of novels particularly appropriate, and it has the further advantage of being more nearly self-explanatory than 'skeleton-novels', as well as suggesting a connection with the more familiar concept of the psychological novel. Psychological elements certainly abound in the *nivolas*, but as presented in the caricaturized personalities of the central characters they are largely abstract and serve to illustrate the general problem of development of the human psyche through examples of failure of such development.

[9] See my essay, 'The Novelistic Logos in Unamuno's *Amor y pedagogía*', *MLN*, 82 (1969), 248-68. A number of interesting comments on the structure of this novel, its relation to *Niebla*, and the thematic significance of its appended treatise on the *pajaritas de papel* are to be found in J.E. Varey, '*Maese Miguel*: Puppets as a Literary Theme in the Work of Unamuno', in *Spanish Thought and Letters in the Twentieth Century*, ed. Germán Bleiberg and E. Inman Fox (Nashville: Vanderbilt University Press, 1966), pp.559-72. For another discussion of the *nivola*, in this case in relation to *Abel Sánchez*, see the Critical Guide by Nicholas G. Round (London: Grant and Cutler, 1974).

It seems appropriate, then, to follow Ribbans in dividing Unamuno's novels into three groups: first the historical novel *Paz en la guerra*, then the two *nivolas*, and finally the novels of passion. Such grouping would also correspond to three distinct chronological periods in the author's work if like most critics we omit the short stories of *El espejo de la muerte*, the social and literary commentary of the *Vida de Don Quijote y Sancho*, and *Cómo se hace una novela* from consideration in establishing a typology of the novels. On the other hand, if like Unamuno we include them, or try to account for them as being in some way related to the novels, we shall have to see the groups as purely thematic categories rather than corresponding also to chronological periods, associating the stories and the *Vida* with the character studies in the third group, as anticipations of the novels of passion, and viewing *Cómo se hace una novela* as a late and final *nivola*.

As for the relations between *Amor y pedagogía* and *Niebla*, there are, to be sure, very clear similarities between Apolodoro Carrascal in the first *nivola* and Augusto Pérez in the second, between their mothers, Marina and Soledad, between the old philosophers, Fulgencio Entrambosmares and Don Fermín, and even between the latters' domineering wives, Edelmira and Ermelinda (whose names are virtually anagrams). But the most important similarity is doubtless that of the central characters' failure to achieve the status of autonomous personalities, which in both cases leads to suicide.

There are, however, important differences between them as well, the most important of which implies the possibility of establishing yet another kind of division among the novels, cutting across that of the three groups thus far identified, as if along another dimension. The basis of this division is that made by Carlos Blanco Aguinaga (*16*) between an *Unamuno agónico*, who struggles to affirm and differentiate his individual being from any total, pure, or infinite being, and an *Unamuno contemplativo*, one of calm reflection and surrender to the infinite, whether in the world of nature or beyond it. The manifestations of this dichotomy are many and varied, beginning with the famous distinction between *historia* and *intra-historia* which Unamuno made in the essays of *En torno al casticismo* (1895). The world of *historia* is seen as one of negation and discontinuity, and its violent conflicts have the effect of differentiating and opposing individuals and nations, while the world of *intra-historia* is regarded as one of affirmation and presence, of eternal continuity and the subordination of differentiated beings to undifferentiated Being. The contrast between these two worlds in Unamuno's thinking has led to a basic conflict in his sentiments between what Blanco Aguinaga and other critics have called the desire to *serse* and the desire to *serlo todo*, the first having the attraction of being determinate and concrete but finite, while the second has the attraction of being limitless both in time and in space, but for that very reason threatens to engulf the specific and individual.[10]

In Unamuno's novels this opposition manifests itself principally in the contrast between maternal and paternal figures, with the mother and symbols of motherhood such as home, church, and nature itself evoking the continuity of pure being, while paternal figures evoke the discontinuity and conflict of the struggle to differentiate and distinguish the self — the struggle to *serse*. When viewed in chronological series the novels seem to be dominated alternately by maternal and paternal figures, in a kind of dialectic which reaches a final synthesis in *San Manuel Bueno, mártir*, in which the saintly priest is called 'aquel varón *matriarcal*' (1129).[11] In the context of such a dialectic the fundamental difference between *Amor y pedagogía* and *Niebla* can be seen in the fact that in the first *nivola* the central figure is dominated by a fully differentiated father who is determined to make his son even more differentiated — that is, distinguished — by educating him to be a hero of the scientific intellect, but who in the process deprives him of human substance, while in

[10] It is important to note that the pure, infinite being of the *serlo todo* is often felt by Unamuno to be equivalent to pure nothingness, precisely because both are totally lacking in limits and therefore in determinate existence (see Chapter 6, n.57). For more on the *serse/serlo todo* paradox see François Meyer, *L'Ontologie de Miguel de Unamuno* (Paris: Presses Universitaires de France, 1955).

[11] For more on *San Manuel, Bueno, mártir*, see the Critical Guide by J.W. Butt (London: Grant and Cutler, 1981). A more detailed discussion of the dialectic mentioned here is in my study, '*Amor y pedagogía* en la dialéctica interior de Unamuno', in *Actas del Tercer Congreso Internacional de Hispanistas* (México: El Colegio de México, 1970), pp.649-56.

Niebla we have a son so dominated by the love of a mother who before her death had been almost literally all the world to him that she remains in his consciousness as a constant, misty presence from which he is never able to free himself. He is therefore a kind of misty presence himself, never fully differentiated from the mist of pure presence which constantly surrounds him.

This survey of the novels of Unamuno has, I hope, served to establish a broad context within which *Niebla* may be understood in its similarities to and differences from the other novels and as occupying a central place in his work, not only chronologically but also in terms of the structure of his thought concerning the nature of literature and of human life itself. Having come at the end of this survey to a discussion of some basic aspects of plot, character, and theme in *Niebla*, I shall now consider each of them in greater detail, beginning in the following chapter with the novel's plot, seen as one aspect of a broader question of structure within the entire work.

2. Problems of structure

The literary criticism of this century has identified a variety of distinctive patterns of narrative structure which give significant form to what might otherwise appear to be a flat chronicle of events narrated in a purely sequential fashion, with little sense of a meaningful relation among them. E.M. Forster has taught us, for example, to see what he calls the 'hour glass' pattern in the kinds of reversal occurring in a novel like Henry James's *The Ambassadors*, and in Hispanic studies Leon Livingstone has shown the importance of the phenomena of mirroring and symmetry to which he gives the name 'interior duplication'.[12]

In *Niebla* the central narrative is the life story of Augusto Pérez, principally in the relatively short period between his reaching adulthood and his death while still a young man. The structure of the narrative is primarily that of the sequence of events constituting his own life's experiences, and we may therefore regard it as a *Bildungsroman*, or novel concerned with the protagonist's development through successive 'stages on life's way'.[13]

Let us begin, then, to examine the structure of *Niebla* in the most immediate and usual sense of the term, as the sequence of events constituting the plot. I assume that the reader of this study is already familiar with the novel, but this survey of its plot is an essential introduction to any interpretation of its basic structural features.

The text begins with a *Prólogo* and a *Post-prólogo*, which do

[12] Forster, *Aspects of the Novel* (London: Edward Arnold; New York: Harcourt Brace, 1927), Chapter 8, 'Pattern and Rhythm'. Livingstone, 'Interior Duplication and the Problem of Form in the Modern Spanish Novel', *PMLA*, 73 (1958), 393-406.

[13] I here evoke the title of a work of Kierkegaard published in 1845, a year after *The Concept of Dread* and a year before the *Concluding Unscientific Postscript*. Judging by the number of underlinings and marginal notes in his own copies of a Danish edition of Kierkegaard's works, it is clear that Unamuno knew all three works extremely well.

not, of course, present the first events in the narrative, but both are inseparable from the novel itself. The *Prólogo*, we discover, is the work of one Víctor Goti, a fictional character who tells us he is a friend of Augusto Pérez. He also shows himself to be well acquainted with Unamuno, however, and the greater part of the prologue is devoted to the exposition of Unamuno's thought on a wide variety of topics, ranging from the Spanish public's reaction to his work to the problem of human mortality. It also includes a discussion of Unamuno's attitudes toward literary genres and tells of the author's ambition to realize a synthesis of tragedy and farce, in terms which suggest that *Niebla* is intended to be just such a synthesis. The *Prólogo* ends with Goti's saying that he disagrees with the version of Augusto's death given by Unamuno, since he believes it was a real case of suicide.

Unamuno replies in the *Post-prólogo* that he would like to dispute this and a number of other affirmations by Goti, but he prefers to leave to him the entire responsibility for what he has said. He does, however, protest at Goti's publishing his opinions about the Spanish reading public, and as for the claim that Augusto's death did not occur in the way Unamuno tells it — that is, as a result of the author's freely made decision — he calls it one of those opinions which merit no more than a smile.

It is therefore clear that although the prologues do not begin the narrative, they are directly related to it and anticipate its ending. They also anticipate the novel's play of juxtapositions with the planes of fiction and reality, for when Goti informs us that the book tells the history of the mysterious death of his friend, Augusto Pérez, we might at first believe that the 'history' is one of real events, but Unamuno undermines the historicity and even the verisimilitude of such a history by this assertion that the death resulted from his own decision as author.

A third prologue, prepared for the edition of 1935, has already been the basis for my comments on the place of *Niebla* in Unamuno's work as a whole. It does not have the same kind of inner relation to the narrative as the first two, but all editions now include it. The third prologue's perspective on the novel is adopted from a much greater distance than that of the others, and from a position entirely external to it. But it does have an

important structural function in introducing another plane
mediating between the external — extra-textual — plane of what
is everyday reality for the reader and the internal — intra-textual
— plane of fictional reality. Between the two is the reality of the
author, normally assumed to be a part of the same historical
reality as that of the reader, but in the first two prologues
partially displaced into the plane of fictional reality by the
presentation of an author who converses and disputes with his
own characters. The introduction of a more external plane of
reality in the new prologue heightens our sense of continuity
between planes and therefore of the possibility of fusion and
confusion between them.

The main narrative begins with the abruptness of the raising
of a curtain as Augusto Pérez appears in the doorway of his
house to go out for a stroll.[14] Almost immediately he finds
himself following an attractive young lady all the way to her
house, where he learns that her name is Eugenia Domingo del
Arco, that she is a piano teacher, and that she lives with an aunt
and uncle (Chapter i).

After writing a letter declaring his admiration for her (ii), he
learns from her reply that she is already engaged, but he decides
to struggle to win her nevertheless (v). As he is passing in front
of her house one day, a bird-cage falls from Eugenia's balcony.
He returns it and introduces himself to the aunt and uncle, doña
Ermelinda and don Fermín, telling them of his interest in their
niece (vi). A few days later he again goes to call and is able to
meet Eugenia. She treats him coldly, but he is all the more
enchanted by what he sees as her strength of character (viii).
Eugenia resents her aunt's presenting him as a good match
because of his wealth and tells her fiancé, Mauricio, that he must
find work so they may be married, or else she will work to
support them both (ix).

When Augusto again comes to call, Eugenia repeats that she is
already engaged to be married, but he insists he has no
pretensions other than being allowed to come occasionally to

[14] Carlos Blanco Aguinaga has emphasized the significance of Augusto's
sudden appearance at the door of his house, particularly as indicated by the fact
that the first words of the narrative are 'Al aparecer Augusto a la puerta de su
casa...' (*28*).

enjoy her presence. When she leaves he decides to sacrifice himself for her happiness by paying up the mortgage on a house she owns so that she may receive the income from it (xi). At the same time he has found that since falling in love with Eugenia he is much more aware of all women, and the next day (xii) he suddenly finds himself attracted to Rosario, the laundry girl who regularly comes to his house.

A few days later Eugenia appears at his house and tells him indignantly she has learned that he has bought her mortgage. She accuses him of trying to make her dependent on him or of trying to buy her affection (xiii). He insists his motives are disinterested and later tells her aunt (xv) that he has given up all hope of winning Eugenia and will even find Mauricio a good job so he will not have to live on her income. Eugenia again goes to see her fiancé and tells him that if he does not find work she may become desperate enough to accept Augusto's dishonourable gift. He says he thinks it is an excellent idea to do so, and even adds that, since having to work has no appeal whatever for him, it might actually be best to marry Augusto for his money and continue their relationship on the side. She becomes completely furious with him and returns home in tears (xvi).

Augusto now sees himself as definitively rejected by Eugenia and seeks to console himself with Rosario. He plans to make a long journey and asks her to go with him, which she promises to do (xviii). A few days later, however, Ermelinda comes to tell him Eugenia now recognizes the rectitude of his intentions, and to show the sincerity of her repentance she is willing to accept the gift, provided it is without obligation of any kind (xix). He suspects Eugenia's motives but tells Ermelinda he accepts her explanations and will be Eugenia's friend, but nothing more than a friend. A few days later Eugenia herself comes to call (xx) and tells him that her acceptance of the gift does not mean she will now accept him in marriage, but her insistence on this point makes him suspect that she is actually trying to get him to renew his proposal. Although feeling trapped, he is close to doing just that when Liduvina suddenly announces the arrival of Rosario. Eugenia realizes there must be some intimacy between Augusto and Rosario and departs in haste. Rosario warns him that

Eugenia is trying to deceive him, and he is very moved by this evidence of loyalty and concern for him.

Finding that his interest in women has grown to such an extent that he is even falling in love with his middle-aged cook, Augusto decides to make woman an object of scientific study and goes to consult the learned Antolín S. Paparrigópulos, a specialist in the subject (xxiii). A part of Augusto's interest in the study is due to his belief that it will help him choose between Eugenia and Rosario, but Paparrigópulos insists that he take three women as objects of study. He decides his cook, Liduvina, could be the third.

To begin the experiment he decides to pretend to woo Eugenia again (xxii), but while he is still thinking about it Rosario arrives, and he begins to experiment on her, making love with a passion which brings them close to sexual intimacy. Rosario seems quite willing, but his passion suddenly fades and he sends her away. He later goes to discuss his dilemma with Víctor (xxv), who advises him simply to marry without worrying too much about which woman he chooses. At the end of this chapter the author addresses the reader directly, commenting that he is amused to see his characters reasoning in such a way as to justify their author's actions while thinking they were justifying their own.

Augusto then goes to try his experiment on Eugenia, but she does, in fact, accept his renewed proposal (xxvi). At first he feels trapped but soon looks forward to the marriage as a means of realizing authentic existence. Eugenia tells him one day that Mauricio has been pursuing her and threatening to compromise her unless she finds some kind of position for him (xvii). She says she thinks it would be best to find him something quite far away so he will stop bothering her. Augusto agrees and does, in fact, find him such a position. Before departing to take up the appointment Mauricio comes to thank Augusto and tells him Rosario is going with him, hinting also that she has told him about her last encounter with Augusto (xxviii). This makes Augusto feel ridiculous, and he becomes so furious that he starts to strangle Mauricio. His fury is soon overwhelmed by a feeling of helplessness, however, and he lets him go.

Three days before the wedding Augusto receives a letter from Eugenia (xxix) telling him she is leaving with Mauricio as he goes to assume his new post. At first Augusto feels strangely calm but then gives way to tears and to feelings of anger and shame for the ridiculousness of his situation and decides to commit suicide. Before doing so, however, he goes to Salamanca to discuss the matter with Miguel de Unamuno, who has just published an essay containing some comments on suicide which Augusto has read (xxxi). He is astonished to learn that the author knows all about him and his intended suicide. Unamuno tells him he cannot kill himself because he is not really alive, being only a product of his author's imagination and therefore a mere fictional character.

When Augusto suggests that perhaps it is actually Unamuno who does not really exist, the author is so annoyed by this impertinence that he decides not merely to forbid his committing suicide but to kill him himself. This makes Augusto plead for his life, but the author is inflexible. Augusto therefore returns home (xxxii) feeling already near death, but when Liduvina gives him a supper he eats voraciously, crying *Edo, ergo sum!* Finally he is overcome with weakness and asks Domingo to put him to bed. He has a telegram sent to Unamuno. saying 'Se salió con la suya. He muerto' (xxxii, 674), and shortly thereafter he cries out the name of Eugenia and falls dead. The servants call the doctor, and the three exchange opinions concerning the cause of death. The physician first assumes it was a heart attack, but Domingo insists it must have been from excessive eating, while Liduvina thinks he simply took it into his head to die. The doctor then concludes that death resulted from a combined failure of stomach, heart, and head.

The author then tells us (xxxiii) that when he received Augusto's telegram he wondered if he had done the right thing with his character, and even thought of reviving him so he could commit suicide as he wished. That night Augusto appears in a dream to tell him such a thing would be impossible. With a final warning that it might, in fact, be Unamuno who is the fictional being, Augusto disappears into the dark mist of his own — and Unamuno's — unconscious. This final chapter of the narrative

proper is itself a kind of epilogue, but it is followed by the
'Oración fúnebre por modo de epílogo' (bearing no chapter
number), in which Augusto's dog, Orpheo, expresses his grief
for the death of his master and makes a series of comments on
the human condition. The fact that there are, in effect, two
epilogues to the novel seems to imply some difficulty or
reluctance on the author's part to put a definitive end to the
work, in the same way that the protracted epilogue and appendix
to *Amor y pedagogía* had expressed that problem in the earlier
nivola.[15] The chief significance of the two epilogues may,
however, lie in the fact that they balance the two prologues and
could therefore be seen as completing a double framework
within which the narrative proper is enclosed. The function of
the entire frame is, I suggest, implicitly that which has been
pointed out with respect to the two prologues (eventually three,
since the third edition) — that of introducing a number of
transitional or mediating planes of reality between the purely
fictional and textual reality of Augusto Pérez and the immediate
empirical reality of the reader.

One might, to be sure, discuss the aesthetic effectiveness of
this structural strategy, but I think it is motivated by thematic
concerns which are in accord with those of the novel as a
whole.[16] In this respect it is at least as pertinent to the main
narrative as any of the interpolated tales and must be regarded
as an integral part of the work itself.

The foregoing plot summary has accounted for all but nine of
thirty-three chapters of the text, of which six are taken up by
Augusto's discussions with Víctor Goti on the subjects of love,
marriage, and the nature of the human condition, while two
consist chiefly of monologues in which Augusto reflects on his
personal situation and one is devoted entirely to an interpolated

[15] See my study, 'The Novelistic Logos in Unamuno's *Amor y pedagogía*',
MLN, 84 (1969), 248-68.

[16] Geoffrey Ribbans regards the 'Oración fúnebre' and the 'Post-prólogo' as
superfluous and even frivolous additions to the text, which reduce, rather than
enhance, its literary effectiveness (*24*, 139-41). He believes they may be due in
part to an excessive scorn for aesthetic form but the two prologues and the two
epilogues (if one counts Chapter xxxiii as a kind of epilogue in itself) do present a
certain formal symmetry, which, as I shall show, can also be found in a number
of other aspects of the work.

tale told by a friend of Augusto known simply as don Antonio.[17]
The function of these chapters, as well as of the monologues,
conversations with Víctor, and interpolated tales included in
chapters which also advance the narrative, is to provide
moments of reflection, analysis, and thematic development
which alternate with those that advance the plot.

Having at this point completed our survey of the principal
events which form the narrative structure of *Niebla*, I should
like to give a more comprehensive view of that structure by
considering possibilities for grouping the chapters into larger
units and identifying the basic continuities and discontinuities
which convert the pure linearity of narrative discourse into a
significant form. Ribbans's excellent study of the structure of
Niebla distinguishes three principal stages in the story of
Augusto Pérez, which he characterizes in the following terms:

> La primera, que abarca siete apartados, marca el despertar
> a la vida consciente del Augusto protoplásmico del
> principio. La segunda, la más larga (18 apartados: VII-
> XXV), constituye el meollo de la historia. A Augusto ya le
> incumbe decidir entre las varias posibilidades de acción
> que se le presentan, ilustradas por diversas anécdotas. La
> sección termina, cuando por fin se ha compremetido a
> cierta línea de acción, con la irrupción por primera vez del
> *Deus ex machina* que es Unamuno. El desenlace nos lo da
> la tercera parte: la ruptura del noviazgo por Eugenia, la
> visita de Augusto a don Miguel y la muerte de aquél. (*24*,
> 11)

In general I find this analysis convincing, although I am

---

[17] This discussion has omitted all mention of the contents of the interpolated
tales because I devote a separate chapter to them. Here I shall just observe that
these tales vary considerably in the extent to which they constitute digressions
from the narrative line (even though all of them are thematically pertinent to it).
At one extreme is the story of Víctor Goti's marriage and his wife's long-delayed
pregnancy, which does, after all, involve a very important character in the novel
and provides the basis for subsequent discussions between him and Augusto. At
the other extreme are stories like those of don Eloíno and of the *fogueteiro*, who
are mere subjects of stories told by the principal characters to each other.
Between the two extremes are those of Avito Carrascal and don Antonio, who do
appear briefly in the main narrative, but only to tell their own stories.

inclined to see the second section as beginning in Chapter vi, which opens with Augusto's telling himself, 'Tengo que tomar alguna determinación' (vi, 572) and shows him going into action in a way which gains him admission to Eugenia's house and establishes his status as a suitor for her hand.[18] This gives the chapter the character of a new beginning which logically goes with the events which immediately derive from it. In any case I believe Ribbans is entirely justified in seeing the first section as presenting the existentialist theme of *compromiso* — involvement with life. This involvement and even Augusto's awareness of life develops only gradually. After his first sight of Eugenia (i), in which he really notices only her eyes, their paths again cross three times before he actually is introduced to her in the second section of the novel. The first time (ii) he completely fails to notice her; the second time (iv) he becomes aware of her eyes only after she has passed. Only on the third occasion (v) have his awareness and involvement proceeded far enough for him to recognize Eugenia and to take the initiatives in which he engages in the second part.

It must also be granted that the interruption of the narrative by the authorial *yo* at the end of Chapter xxv is a major discontinuity, which can be seen as bringing the central section to a close and giving prominence to what I should call the meta-novelistic themes, which dominate the end of the work — that is, the themes concerned with the nature of the novel, and with the relation of fiction to reality itself. At the same time, of course, the final section brings to a climax the tragic story of Augusto Pérez, and in his death the existential and meta-novelistic themes finally converge.

This analysis of the structure of *Niebla* in terms of the development of Augusto's character and the author's attitude toward him as a product of his own creative imagination is, I believe, entirely valid on the level of what might be called the existential structure of the work, but it is a mark of the

[18] There is a slight contradiction in the passage here quoted from Ribbans, probably due to a typographical error, in that we are told the first section consists of seven chapters, but later that the second section begins with chapter vii. In terms of the general character of this analysis it makes little difference how the passage is emended.

complexity of *Niebla* that it presents a number of different levels on which convincing structural analyses may be made. The most fundamental of these is one that might be called the level of textual structure — understanding the term as referring to the order in which the narrator introduces the characters, recounts the events of the plot and the interpolated tales, and distributes them among the 34 sections (33 chapters plus the epilogue) of the narrative text.

In the most immediate terms this level of structure may be identified by the position of the five interpolated tales among these 34 sections.[19] The tale of don Avito Carrascal occurs in Chapter xiii, that of Víctor Goti in xiv; the story of don Eloíno is in xvii, and those of don Antonio and the *fogueteiro* are in xxi and xxii respectively. This arrangement makes for a perfectly symmetrical division of the novel into three parts, consisting of 12, 10, and 12 chapters (counting the 'Oración fúnebre a modo de epílogo' as a final chapter), and within the central section an essential symmetry is effected by the placing of the five tales in the first two and the last two chapters of the section, with one approximately in the middle — that is, in the fifth of the ten chapters — thus producing a 2-1-2 arrangement in the sequence. The central section of this symmetrically structured novel is therefore itself symmetrically structured — a symmetry within symmetry.

The internal unity of the first section of twelve chapters is provided by its function as beginning or introduction, in which a presentation is made of all the principal characters and the basic themes are set forth.[20] These include such existential problems as what it is to exist authentically, what it is to be really in love,

[19] In addition to the five relatively extensive tales, this section also contains two paragraph-length anecdotes, which are certainly interpolations, and are similar to the tales in illustrating various aspects of inter-personal relations. The first is Eugenia's story of Martín Rubio and don Emérito in xv, and the second is Augusto's anecdote about a personal experience, told in xix. It is interesting to note that this placement makes them equidistant from the central tale (that of don Eloíno) in xvii. This makes them participate in the approximate symmetry of placement of the longer interpolations, but because of the brevity of these anecdotes, I exclude them from consideration here.

[20] The entire section can be regarded as conforming to the Aristotelian definition of the Beginning of a literary work, that is, as 'that which is not itself necessarily after anything else, and which has naturally something else after it' (*Poetics*, VII).

and what the goal of life may be, as well as the literary problem of the relation between fiction and reality and the metaphysical question as to why there are any beings at all rather than nothing.

The unity of the central section is provided by its development of these themes, largely with the help of the case histories which the interpolated tales present. At the same time, however, it advances the plot in a number of essential respects. The section begins with the visit to Augusto by Eugenia, whose rejection of the gift of the mortgage is also a rejection of him. Later, however, she becomes even more angry with Mauricio for suggesting that she marry Augusto but continue her relations with him (xvi) and finally she sends word through her aunt (xix) that she will accept the gift after all. This does, then, prepare the way for a basic reversal in the action, but since by this time the rejected Augusto has begun to be interested in Rosario, the effect of this restoration of his relations with Eugenia is to create an equilibrium in his position with respect to both young women. The final two chapters in this section (xxi and xxii) reinforce the static quality of this equilibrium by being completely devoted to the presentation of interpolated material which presents new perspectives on love and marriage but does nothing in immediate terms to further a solution of Augusto's problems.

The final section begins by recalling the condition in which he found himself before hearing the final two interpolated tales. He is described as being 'como el asno de Buridán, entre Eugenia y Rosario' (xxiii, 636), but immediately thereafter he is shown beginning to move out of this position at dead center by taking action to choose one of them as the wife who will give reality to his existence.[21] Beginning as the series of experiments in feminine psychology undertaken after consultation with Antolín S. Paparrigópulos, these actions end in failure and lead ultimately to Augusto's suicide/death/disappearance at the end of the novel. The ambiguity with which his death is here

---

[21] The principal existentialist themes of *Niebla*, and their parallels with and possible influences from Kierkegaard, have been discussed by Ribbans (*24*) and Ruth House Webber (*34*). See also Wyers (*35*). I shall discuss Augusto's efforts to give reality to his existence at greater length in the following chapter.

presented (an ambiguity anticipated in the different versions given in the *Prólogo* and the *Post-prólogo*) gives expression in the narrative to the questions of the relation of fiction to reality, of author to work, and of language, thought, and consciousness to physical existence.

The symmetry observed in the placement of the interpolated tales and in the three-part structure of the novel also manifests itself in a number of other ways. Consider, for example, the structure implicit in Augusto's ideas about human life and death expressed in one of the early monologues:

> Por debajo de esta corriente de nuestra existencia, por dentro de ella, hay otra corriente en sentido contrario; aquí vamos del ayer al mañana, allí se va del mañana al ayer... Las entrañas de la historia son una contrahistoria, es un proceso inverso al que ella sigue. El río subterráneo va del mar a la fuente... (vii, 578)[22]

A similar concept of reversal appears in Augusto's concept of what happens to human consciousness after death:

> Cuando morimos nos da la muerte media vuelta en nuestra órbita y emprendemos la marcha hacia atrás, hacia el pasado, hacia lo que fue. Y así, sin término, devanando la madeja de nuestro destino... (vii, 578)

In death the experiences of our lives continue to pass through our consciousness, but in reverse order. What is more, even in life we are aware of a constant inner flow of time in a direction opposite to that of our conscious existence. In both cases the river of time is conceived of as flowing from sea to source, rather than — or at the same time as — from source to sea. It may not seem immediately evident that such a reversal implies a

[22] Readers of Unamuno's *En torno al casticismo* will, of course, recall that the first of those essays (1895) had invented the term *intrahistoria* as an alternate name for the eternal tradition which he regarded as the substance of the external phenomena of history. In general the concept of *intrahistoria* seems much more static than that of *contrahistoria*, but the suggestion that *historia* and *contrahistoria* move in a constantly repeated cycle makes the contrast less striking than one might at first believe.

symmetrical structure, but analysing the actual language used to express the concept we see that it is basically a chiasmus, a syntactic structure in which two or more words appear in a given order and are then repeated in reverse order. Using Augusto's image of *mar* and *fuente*, we can say that the structure of the concept of *contrahistoria* can be represented in the form *fuente—mar: mar—fuente*, or to use another figure often occurring in Unamuno's thought, *cuna—tumba: tumba—cuna*.[23] When put in a form in which the entire structure can be simultaneously perceived, its symmetrical nature becomes clear.

An even more significant instance of symmetry and chiastic reversal occurs in the sequential structure of Augusto's relations with the three women with whom he decides to attempt his psychological experiment. The first woman whom Augusto and the reader encounter in the course of the narrative is Eugenia, but we soon learn that before that the principal female figures in his life had been his cook, Liduvina, and his mother. The death of his mother has occurred some six months before the beginning of the narrative, but Augusto's frequent invocation of her name makes it clear that she is constantly present in his thoughts.[24]

[23] In *Cómo se hace una novela*, for example, he recalls his exile in Paris as a time when 'pesaban sobre mí inefables recuerdos inconscientes de ultra-cuna', and adds that 'nuestra desesperada esperanza de una vida personal de ultra-tumba se alimenta y medra de esa vaga remembranza de nuestro arraigo en la eternidad de la historia' (VIII, 709). In many cases Unamuno does not make explicit the complete chiastic structure, but it is clearly implicit in the contrast between what the reader knows to be the normal order of relations and the kind of reversal with which he presents us. Thus, when Augusto says that the subterranean river flows from *mar* to *fuente*, the reader naturally contrasts this with his knowledge that in nature the flow is from *fuente* to *mar*.

[24] At the beginning of ii we are told it is six months, and at the end of iv that it is two years since his mother died. Ribbans believes (*24*, 118) that this means eighteen months have passed between the two chapters, but he also quotes a letter from Unamuno to Warner Fite which seems to acknowledge that the discrepancy is an authorial lapse. The difficulty in assuming so long an interval between the two chapters is that all of the first five chapters give every appearance of being part of a continuous temporal sequence. Only at the beginning of vi does it seem uncertain how much time has passed since the end of the preceding chapter. In any case it is clear that ever since her death she has been constantly present in Augusto's thought. The significance of the mother as presence-in-absence is effectively pointed out by Carlos Blanco Aguinaga in *16* and in his essay, 'La madre, su regazo y el 'sueño de dormir' en la obra de Unamuno', *Cuadernos de la Cátedra Miguel de Unamuno*, 7 (1956), 69-84.

Rosario, as we have seen, appears for the first time in Chapter xii, which in this analysis brings the first part of the novel to a close. She also appears near the beginning of the third part, as the first of the women who are to be subjects of the proposed psychological experiments. The experiment with Rosario ends with Augusto's failure to achieve a loving relationhip with her, and he then turns to Eugenia, who has all along presumably been the principal object of his amorous interest. This attempt to find authentic love also fails when she leaves him for Mauricio, and after deciding to commit suicide he returns home, where Liduvina prepares him his final meal, one so enormous that it appears one possible cause of his death may simply be that of overeating.

The significance of Augusto's last meal and its consequences has been aptly pointed out by Alexander Parker:

> In the course of his search for 'knowledge', experience had shown Augusto that love is expressed in speech and that all speech is lying deception. By stuffing himself with food, he is turning himself into 'the physiological man', abdicating speech and thought, and seeking to return to his mother's womb: '...undress me completely, completely', he says to his servant. 'Leave me as my mother brought me into the world, as I was born — if indeed I was ever born... lay me down now. I want you yourself to lay me on the bed, for I can't move'. (*32*, 135)

The suggestion that death is a kind of return to the mother's womb, in what Unamuno on occasion called a *desnacer*,[25] or mirror-image of birth, implies the possibility of adding the mother to both ends of the chronological sequence of women in Augusto's life. The whole structure of Augusto's relations with the women in his life may therefore be expressed in the scheme:

---

[25] In *Amor y pedagogía*, for example, don Fulgencio Entrambosmares says, '...así como nuestro morir es un *des-nacer*, nuestro nacer es un *des-morir*...' (II, 339).

(Madre) (Liduvina) Eugenia Rosario : Rosario Eugenia Liduvina (Madre)

(Madre),

where parentheses are used to indicate the presences which are implicit realities in Augusto's experience, even though not presented in this order in the text. The mother also appears below the line, to indicate that she is a timeless presence throughout, in contrast to the temporal sequence implied by the series shown above the line.

The order in which Augusto encounters these women would seem, of course, to be purely fortuitous (except for his mother, naturally), but a kind of rationale for the sequence appears in his reflections on his relations with them, which points toward an implicit theory of the structure of human life and the development of the self. In planning to undertake his psychological research he finally decides to take all three women then in his life as subjects for the experiments, commenting to himself:

> Tengo, pues, tres: Eugenia, que me habla a la imaginación, a la cabeza; Rosario, que me habla al corazón, y Liduvina, mi cocinera, que me habla al estómago. Y cabeza, corazón y estómago son las tres facultades del alma que otros llaman inteligencia, sentimiento y voluntad. Se piensa con la cabeza, se siente con el corazón y se quiere con el estómago. ¡Esto es evidente! Y ahora... (xxiv, 643)

The parallels here established between the three women of the narrative and three basic aspects of the self suggest the possibility of transforming our scheme in such a way as to reveal two additional versions of the structure. In terms of the bodily self, which Augusto here uses as metaphors, the structure becomes:

estómago/cabeza/corazón : corazón/cabeza/estómago.

In terms of faculties of the soul, for which the metaphors presumably stand, the structure is:

voluntad/inteligencia/sentimiento : sentimiento/inteligencia/voluntad.

The fact that Augusto sees a correspondence between faculties of soul or mind and parts of the body, and between these and each of the three women with whom in different ways he is in love, gives his ideas the character of a theory of the structure of mental and emotional development, presented as consisting of three phases. Liduvina, the cook, who comes right after — and just before — the mother in the first structural scheme, has a function which is largely maternal, one of nourishing and nurturing, of satisfying the earliest and most basic of physical needs and instinctual desires. The faculty of soul associated with her and with the demands of the *estómago* is identified as *voluntad*, because this will is the pure and almost undifferentiated desire to maintain physical existence.

If Liduvina, coming at the beginning of Augusto's development, speaks to his most primordial desires, Rosario, who speaks to his heart and sentiment, is the only one of the three who offers the possibility of realizing the desires of mature sexuality. The traditional euphemism which associates such desires with the heart is, of course, generally understood in Western culture as a metonymy by which the true physical basis of those desires is modestly concealed and obliquely revealed. At the same time, to be sure, the heart can be understood as a metaphor for the sentiment of genuine affection which normally accompanies mature sexual desire, making possible the transcendence of self-centered instincts which is essential for the creation of new life.

The significance of Eugenia's place within the structure of Augusto's speculations is much more problematic, just as in the narrative itself Augusto's efforts to satisfy the kind of desire she represents is constantly problematic. His statement that she speaks to his imagination, his head, and his intelligence reminds us of the fact that earlier in the novel one of the questions raised by Víctor Goti which most disturbed him was whether his love for her was merely of the head, and when he decided to buy back the mortgage for her, he clearly expected it to prove that it was also of the heart.

Yet if the desire to which Eugenia speaks is not the sentiment corresponding to what we normally mean by love, we are left with the question as to what desire or desires she does, in fact, speak. Beyond the initial attraction of her eyes, on which Augusto concentrates his attention with virtually no awareness of any other attribute, Augusto encounters very little that would seem capable of attracting him to her. Her attitude toward him is cold at best, and frequently even angry and cruel. It therefore seems to be precisely in this behaviour that at least a partial answer to this question may be found, for if her cruelty verges occasionally on the sadistic, his self-abasement before her is openly masochistic, as when he responds to her anger over his buying the mortgage by saying, '¡Pégame, Eugenia, pégame; insúltame, escúpeme, haz de mí lo que quieras!' (xiii, 598).

At the same time, it must be admitted that Augusto has, in fact, tainted their relationship by his use of money, for despite his protestations of disinterestedness, Eugenia's suspicions of his motives are quite understandable. Although the reader is aware that Augusto is perhaps morally and quite certainly psychologically incapable of the self-interest necessary for actually attempting to win her by making her financially dependent on him, the introduction of a monetary element — perhaps all the more clearly so because of his lack of self-interestedness — has in itself a destructive effect on their relationship. When her attitude toward him changes from one of angry rejection to contemptuous dismissal, it would seem at least in part to be because she sees him and any relationship with him as contaminated by filthy lucre. In later chapters, when she accepts the gift his money has bought and even consents to marry him, it is clear that she acts purely out of self-interest, inspired purely by a calculating *inteligencia*, with no spontaneous sentiment from the *corazón*.

There is, nevertheless, one positive aspect to Augusto's relationship with Eugenia — and therefore to the stage of mental and emotional development to which she corresponds. This is the emergence of an awareness of self, of knowledge of one's own identity, and of a sense of purpose in life. Convinced that he has fallen completely in love with her, he says that her eyes 'me hacen creer que existo, ¡dulce ilusión! *Amo, ergo sum!*' (vii, 578), and faced with the task of winning her from his as yet unknown rival, he can exclaim, 'Ya tiene mi vida una finalidad: ya tengo una conquista que llevar a cabo' (ii, 563). Even the very pain he feels from being finally abandoned by her contributes to his consciousness of self: '¡ahora sí, ahora me siento, ahora me palpo, ahora no dudo de mi existencia real!' (xxx, 664). The strength of Eugenia's own ego, which Augusto admires as her 'recia independencia de carácter' (viii, 581), is completely unproblematic, and rather than being shown as emerging and developing, it appears as a fixed essence of the quality of personality which Augusto is striving to achieve.

Yet if Eugenia appears in herself to be free of inner conflict, it is clear that the stage of development represented by Augusto's relationship to her is the most paradoxical and problematic of the three. On one hand the love that speaks to the *inteligencia* seems clearly to correspond to the noblest and highest of the faculties of mind, just as, in physical terms, the *cabeza* is the highest of the parts with which Augusto relates the three faculties and the three women. On the other hand, the cruelty and contempt with which Eugenia treats him, his own self-abasement before her, and the suggestion that Augusto's morally ambiguous gift of money is virtually the material embodiment of both her cruelty and his self-abasement imply the opposite of the noblest and the highest in human character and human relationships.[26]

[26] Readers of Freud may notice certain parallels between the theory of a three-stage development in the human mind and emotions which I believe is implicit in Augusto's relations with the three women and the psychoanalytic theory of libido development. Most of the differences, such as Augusto's relating the first stage (which for him becomes also the last stage) to the stomach (whereas Freud calls it an oral stage) present no great problem. For the second stage the parallels may be less convincing, but Freud's conception of it as 'characterized by the predominance of *sadism*' is, certainly, an important parallel. Finally, for the stage to which Rosario corresponds Freud's frankly sexual terminology must be recognized as identifying at least a part (even though not actually fulfilled) of the reality of the relationship Augusto has with her. See 'Three Essays on the Theory of Sexuality' (1905), in *The Standard Edition of the Complete Psychological Works of Sigmund Freud*, ed. James Strachey (London: Hogarth Press, 1974), VII, pp.123-243. Particularly helpful for an outline of the theory is p.233 in the final 'Summary'. The possibility of actual influence from Freud on Unamuno's thought is highly unlikely, but that the novelist and the psychiatrist may have had similar intuitions concerning the human mind and the emotions is most

In summary, then, I believe it is possible to interpret the essentially symmetrical structures of *Niebla* as representing a series of ascending stages in the maturing of Augusto's desires, both in their physical and in their psychological aspects. The maternal Liduvina corresponds to the basic — and essentially infantile — desire for the nourishment to sustain the physical being, and therefore for that being itself. The relationship to Eugenia corresponds to a desire for an aggressive affirmation of the ego, the self as conscious of its own separate existence, even though it be at the expense of the physical being (as in Augusto's initial self-abasement and eventual desire for suicide). In contrast to the passively received nourishment which is the material expression of desire in the first stage, the preoccupation in the second stage is with that which is deliberately yielded by the self — symbolically represented in this case by Augusto's money — as a material means by which the separateness of the self is maintained. Finally, the relationship to Rosario, although seeming to be much less significant than the one with Eugenia, is shown by this analysis to correspond, in fact, to the highest of the three stages, in which the desire for mature sexual love subsumes all aspects of material and physical desire in the tender sentiments of authentic love, the love and desire which are *de corazón*. This is the desire which is intrinsically self-transcending, moving beyond concern for sustenance of the physical self and beyond affirmation of the conscious self to concern for an authentically loved other, and ultimately to the creation of new life. If Rosario's role in *Niebla* is a secondary one, and if Augusto's attempt to realize the kind of desire which she represents ends in failure, it is doubtless because he has in fact never fully transcended the first two stages, and because this particular novel is concerned with the difficulties which beset its protagonist in affirming his existence as a separate and conscious self.

After the failure of his experiment with Rosario, Augusto begins a process of descent through the two previous stages in

certainly not. In any case I do not wish to imply that the purely psychological themes of *Niebla* — whether Freudian in formulation or not — are the primary ones. They are, rather, simply a part of the broader questions of existence and being with which the novel is concerned.

reverse order, but here, too, he encounters failure. The love which is purely *de cabeza*, and therefore devoid of genuine sentiment, can never lead to authentic existence, particularly when such aggressive negativity accompanies it, and the effort to achieve it by returning to Liduvina and eating his enormous last meal is also utterly futile. The belief that he can attain it by turning into the physiological man is purely illusory, since physiological reality, however basic, is far from the whole of human reality, and for a character of fiction, moreover, physiological reality is forever impossible.

After Augusto's death the discussion between the doctor, who first believes it was from heart failure, and the two servants, one of whom believes it was due to indigestion — a failure of the stomach — while the other believes it was *de la cabeza*, simply a matter of getting it in his head that he was going to die, is finally resolved by the doctor's conclusion that 'este señor don Augusto ha muerto de las tres cosas, de todo el cuerpo, por síntesis' (xxxii, 676). Whether it was a matter of suicide is left unresolved, but the correspondences established by Augusto between Liduvina, Eugenia, and Rosario, on the one hand, and *estómago*, *cabeza*, and *corazón* on the other hand, clearly suggest that the final diagnosis is a metaphor for Augusto's failure in existential terms, the failure to realize authentic love and authentic existence for himself.

The process of descent which begins, following his failure with Rosario, therefore leads to his final disappearance 'en la niebla negra' (xxxiii, 678), and the reversal of order produces the chiastic structure on the level of character and interpersonal relations. The mid-point of this structure does not, of course, correspond to that of the purely textual structure I have pointed out in the 12-10-12 grouping of the chapters and in the placing of the interpolated tales within the central section. The thematic significance of that structure is largely a meta-novelistic one, since the placing of Víctor Goti's discussion of his *nivola* at the center of that structure (xvii) and the placing of various other examples of story-telling symmetrically around it make the problem of novel-writing and of narrating one of the central concerns of this novel. Ultimately, however, as I hope to show in subsequent chapters, the two themes are inseparable, since for Unamuno the problem of making and affirming the conscious self and the problem of making a novel are basically the same.

In this chapter the study of thematic and narrative structures has proved to be inseparable from the study of the characters of *Niebla*, since the significance of these structures is to be found largely in what they indicate about the characters' interpersonal relationships. This has already required me to make a number of comments about the personalities of many of the characters, but a fuller discussion of the novel's techniques for the representation of character, as well as of all the characters individually, is still essential. The following chapter will therefore be devoted to this discussion.

3. Character and characterization

In this chapter my principal concern will be to discuss the characters of *Niebla* as creations of the art of literary characterization, but it will be useful to consider first some of Unamuno's ideas on human character generally — that is, in real life — since I believe some of them have had an important effect on his way of representing characters in fiction.[27] Let us begin, then, with some of Unamuno's remarks in *Del sentimiento trágico de la vida* on what it is to be a man, an individual human being:

> Ser un hombre es ser algo concreto, unitario y sustantivo, es ser cosa, *res*... Y lo que determina a un hombre, lo que le hace *un hombre*, uno y no otro, el que es y no el que no es, es un principio de unidad y un principio de continuidad. Un principio de unidad, primero, en el espacio, merced al cuerpo... Y un principio de unidad en el tiempo... La memoria es la base de la personalidad individual... (VII, 112-14)

Although the individual personality is here described as *sustantivo*, this does not mean that it is itself a timeless substance or eternal essence. Mankind, for Unamuno, is constituted as a being in time, and he believes that the efforts of theologians, such as Augustine and Aquinas, to prove that the soul is an incorruptible and subsistent substance, are based simply on the desire to prove that this makes it capable of receiving from God the gift of immortality.[28] It is true, he grants, that we have a certain subjective awareness of the

[27] When I speak here of character in general, it is not, of course, in the narrow sense of 'moral character', but in the broad sense of 'personality' or 'mind'.

[28] The arguments of St Thomas Aquinas to which Unamuno refers are in the *Summa theologica*, LXXV, 1-6, where Aquinas takes up many of the arguments advanced by Augustine in *De Trinitate*.

substantial persistence of an inner self despite any changes which occur in our bodies, but the fact that our sense of identity is relatively persistent despite outward physical changes does not, for Unamuno, prove that this inner identity possesses the absolute and eternal permanence of a subsistent, incorruptible substance (VII, 158).

Yet even leaving aside the question as to whether human character and personality subsist beyond the death of the body, we can still recognize the importance of Unamuno's discussion of these matters purely in terms of what it implies with respect to his view of the nature of character and personality in this life. While rejecting traditional arguments in favor of the idea that personalities are immortal, he also rejects any view of them as fixed substances, whose persistence in a given identity is essentially unproblematic.

In contrast to the views of human character which he rejects are those which see it not as fixed but as always in flux, possessing a relatively stable identity derived from its unity in space and continuity in time but no substantial being in itself. In the essay, 'Pirandello y yo', written in response to certain comments on *Niebla* by Italian critics who pointed out the similarity between the Italian dramatist and the Spanish novelist in their treatment of character, Unamuno denied that either he or Pirandello had previously known the other's work but recognized as typical of both of them their 'modo de ver y desarrollar las personas históricas — o sea de ficción — en flujo vivo de contradicciones, como una serie de yos, como un río espiritual. Todo lo contrario de lo que en la dramaturgia tradicional se llama un carácter' (VIII, 502).

This, then, is the essence of Unamuno's conception of character — both in fiction and in life. Philosophically akin to (and partly derived from) the empiricism of Hume but with echoes of Heraclitus as well, it regards the phenomenon of personality as a living flux or a series of momentary selves, and rejects every concept of stable being or substantial selfhood in human character, whether it be in the form of Descartes's *res cogitans* or the subsistent *anima* of Aquinas.[29]

It is clear, however, that in *Niebla*, as in the earlier novel, *Amor y pedagogía*, most of the characters are virtual caricatures, sometimes comical or even grotesque in the extent to which they represent particular human foibles or tendencies in contemporary thought. Notable examples of this in *Niebla* are don Fermín and Antolín S. Paparrigópulos, both of whom are incarnations of different kinds of ideological pedantry, of the left and right respectively, but even when not exaggerated to the point of caricature most of the other characters are also recognizable as types of one kind or another. This does seem to contradict Unamuno's statements about developing his characters in an essentially fluid way, since the typical and the grotesque usually imply a substantially fixed identity, if not in a sense very similar to Aquinas's concept of the substantial 'soul', certainly in one quite different from any view of human character as a 'río espiritual'.

I shall return to the problem of this apparent contradiction at the end of this chapter, upon completion of this survey of the principal characters of the novel, but I have introduced it by speaking of the tendency toward caricature because such a tendency is clearly related to one of the most striking and immediately perceptible aspects of the novel as a whole: the creation of names which symbolize or in some other way signify something about each character's personality, condition, or position in the structure of interpersonal relations. In Chapter 1 of this study I mentioned this as one of the defining characteristics of the *nivola* generally, adding it to Geoffrey Ribbans's criteria for identifying *Amor y pedagogía* and *Niebla* as the two works which constitute that sub-genre, and suggesting that it might help to justify the inclusion of *Cómo se hace una novela* among the *nivolas* also. The creation of names of this kind, which German literary critics refer to as *redende Namen* — literally, 'speaking names', names which in themselves say something about the persons who bear them — is a familiar

---

[29] *Summa theologica*, LXXV, 1-6. The thought of Descartes on soul or mind as a thinking substance, in contrast to every material body, or *res extensa*, is summarized in his *Principia philosophiae*, I, lxiii.

procedure in prose fiction, and it is used even by such masters of
realism as Galdós, Dickens, and Trollope in the creation of fully
rounded, realistic characters. Yet it must be admitted that it is a
procedure which readily implies — and leads the reader to expect
— an element of caricature in the character so named.

One of the clearest examples of this procedure in Unamuno is
that of don Avito Carrascal, who appears briefly in *Niebla* as the
teller of the first of the interpolated tales but had also been seen
in *Amor y pedagogía* as one of the central characters. The
significance of this name may not, perhaps, be obvious to every
reader, but those who know Unamuno's essays on *Don Quijote*
will recall that he regarded the bachiller Sansón Carrasco as the
essence of unimaginative common sense. In *Amor y pedagogía*
don Avito Carrascal is a person of the most complete *hábito
carrascal*, the most egregiously pedestrian rationality in relation
to all the great questions of life. In *Niebla* he appears as a tragic
and therefore far profounder figure, but his name is a constant
reminder of his previous state of mind.

The name of Augusto Pérez does not involve such literal
wordplay, but some reflection shows that this, too, is a
profoundly significant name. Like the Alejandro Gómez of
Nada menos que todo un hombre, the hero of *Niebla* has a given
name suggesting heroic grandeur and imperial distinction,
combined with a most undistinguished surname suggesting
origins in the indeterminate mass of society's lower classes.[30]
The comic irony of his name is made clear in the very first
sentences of the novel, and although we do not learn his
surname until later in the chapter, the contrast between the
distinction implied by 'Augusto' and the unheroic reality of his
character is immediately evident:

Al aparecer Augusto a la puerta de su casa extendió el
brazo derecho, con la mano palma abajo y abierta, y
dirigiendo los ojos al cielo quedóse un momento parado en
esta actitud estatuaria y augusta. No era que tomaba

[30] A notable example of a tendency to identify the name Pérez with a kind of
Ortegan *hombre-masa* is to be found in Jorge Guillén's poem 'Potencia de
Pérez', which satirically portrays Francisco Franco as a pure 'Pérez', totally
lacking in distinction.

posesión del mundo exterior, sino que observaba si llovía.
(i, 557)

The occurrence of 'Augusto' near the beginning of the first sentence and of 'augusta' at the end points up the ironic pun in his given name, and the reference to his 'actitud estatuaria' suggests that for a moment he resembles a heroic statue of Caesar Augustus.[31] This suggestion is, of course, completely undermined by the explanation that the gesture is really simply the product of a very pedestrian kind of prudence, which subsequently will convince him that he must, indeed, open his umbrella, roll up the bottoms of his trousers, and, when it has stopped raining, carefully spread a newspaper on a park bench before sitting down.

Critical comments on the novel tend for the most part to emphasize the ridiculous incongruity of Augusto's two names, and certainly the comic irony with which he is presented is clearly deliberate. I believe, however, that another, quite serious, dimension of meaning can be seen by comparing Augusto to Alejandro Gómez, whose name is fully as incongruous as Augusto's but lacking completely in comic effect. Blanco Aguinaga has pointed out that the hero of *Nada menos* is a self-made man, who arrives as conqueror (Alejandro) in the world of the bourgeoisie and aristocracy. His plebeian surname is the very symbol of the humble origins he refers to in his proud assertion, 'Yo vengo de la nada' (II, 1024).[32] Unlike Alejandro, who actually is a conqueror and has succeeded in distinguishing himself from the virtually anonymous mass of his origins, Augusto has a name which is ironic because he fails utterly to attain any of his objectives, whether it be the love of Eugenia, the sexual conquest of Rosario, the attainment of his own authentic existence as an autonomous individual, or preservation of that existence itself. Alejandro's success in

---

[31] It is possible Unamuno was thinking specifically of the Augustus of Primaporta, probably the best preserved and most heroic of the original statues of the Emperor. The hand is not precisely 'palma abajo y abierta', but the arm is extended very much as in the description of Augusto.

[32] Carlos Blanco Aguinaga, 'Aspectos dialécticos de las *Tres novelas ejemplares*', *Revista de Occidente*, 2a época, 2, no.19 (1967), 51-70.

differentiating himself from his origins is social and economic. Augusto's problem — and eventual failure — is the profoundly individual (psychological and existential) one of a man who is desperately trying to make and be himself, a determinate individual, differentiated from his origins. The lack of distinction in his background is not that of the social *nada* of the proletariat but simply that of the indeterminacy, for the individual consciousness, of its own origins, since whatever precedes consciousness is obviously beyond it, subsumed in an indeterminate and undifferentiated prior condition of being. In psychological terms the problem of differentiating himself from his own origins is one of achieving emotional independence from his mother. At one point he recalls the years before her death as a time when he literally — as a mental entity, at least — 'formaba parte de su madre y vivía a su amparo' (xiii, 598), and in many ways it seems that all his failures are due to his inability, even after her death, to cease being 'parte de su madre', to differentiate himself as a separately existing individual, as commentaries on the novel have often suggested.[33]

There is, I believe, little doubt that the theme of the problem of differentiating and distinguishing — whether it be the self from its origins, the individual from the mass, or the particular from the general — is a major part of the significance of the references to 'niebla' in *Niebla*. The word first appears in the course of Augusto's reflections on his encounter with Eugenia, when he thinks to himself that 'los hombres no sucumbimos a las grandes penas ni a las grandes alegrías, y es porque...vienen embozadas en una inmensa niebla de pequeños incidentes. Y la vida es esto, la niebla. La vida es una nebulosa' (ii, 561). The minutiae of daily life, its 'pequeños incidentes', are all so much alike and so unremarkable in themselves that they are as indistinguishable as the individual droplets of water which compose a mist or fog, and taken all together they have the further effect of making it difficult for any other object to be distinguished from them.

An important source for Unamuno's use of mist as an image

[33] Most explicitly by Gullón (*19*) and Feal Deibe (*17*), and also by Blanco Aguinaga (*16*).

for Augusto's condition has been identified by Ruth House Webber (*34*, pp.132-33) in a comment by Kierkegaard on the second part of his *Either/Or*, in which his hero has become a husband, thereby rising from the aesthetic to the ethical stage of life: 'Through phantom-like images of the mist, through the distractions of an abundant thought-content..., we win through to an entirely individual human being, existing in the strength of the ethical.'[34] As a source for the image and for the character of Augusto the passage suggested by Webber is quite convincing, since from the very beginning of the novel Unamuno takes pains to emphasize Augusto's purely aesthetic attitudes, his moving about in the world as if among 'phantom-like images of the mist', and the distractions of his 'abundant thought-content'.

His aestheticism, for example, is revealed at the end of the first paragraph, when after finding that it is raining he expresses annoyance at having to use his umbrella: 'Es una desgracia esto de tener que servirse uno de las cosas — pensó Augusto —; tener que usarlas. El uso estropea y hasta destruye toda belleza' (i, 557). That he feels himself living among phantom-like images of mist is clear from the passage I have quoted containing his view of the whole of life as a 'niebla', and the abundance of his thought-content is evident from his numerous monologues, which show him constantly reflecting, analysing and questioning every aspect of his experience. In the monologue in which he engages when first following Eugenia, he himself declares, 'Mi imaginación no descansa' (i, 558).

Thinking is, in fact, Augusto's principal occupation. We learn in Chapter II that he is rich, and later that he has a university degree in law (v, 572), but there is no evidence that he does any kind of work. The narrator's statement that 'Augusto no era un caminante de la vida' (i, 557) proves to be very apt, since aside from the fact that he does not direct his energies — is not a 'caminante' — toward any professional or economic goals, he is at this stage even without any personal goals beyond those of continuing the routine of his daily walk, his 'almuerzo de todos los días' (ii, 561), his visit to the Casino, and his game of chess

[34] *Kierkegaard's 'Concluding Unscientific Postscript'*, trans. David F. Swenson (Princeton: University Press, 1944), pp.226-27.

with Víctor Goti. His aestheticism is, in fact, an actual rejection of goal-directed activity, based as it is on the belief that use destroys beauty. Practical use, after all, relates an object to a finality outside and beyond itself, and the movement toward that finality is realized within the flow of time. Augusto would seem to prefer a timeless world of entities whose only finalities are within themselves. Their only function should be that of being contemplated by thought, in effect being converted into thought themselves.

There are, to be sure, indications early in the novel that love will finally give him some goals in life, especially if he has to struggle for it. When he learns from the *portera* that Eugenia has another *novio*, he exclaims, '¡Lucharemos!... Ya tiene mi vida una finalidad: ya tengo una conquista que llevar a cabo. ¡Oh, Eugenia, mi Eugenia, has de ser mía!' (ii, 563). In terms of the novel's principal metaphor the process of becoming able to discern specific objects and objectives in life is like the condensation of mist into discrete drops of rain or even of its solidification into hailstones. Again, it is love, according to Augusto, that makes this possible: 'Y para amar algo, ¿qué basta? ¡Vislumbrarlo! El vislumbre; he aquí la intuición amorosa, el vislumbre en la niebla. Luego viene el precisarse, la visión perfecta, el resolverse la niebla en gotas de agua o en granizo, o en nieve, o en piedra' (iv, 566). All of this is because, as he had said when declaring all of life to be a mist, Eugenia has suddenly emerged from that mist (ii, 561).

In fact, however, Augusto not only fails ever to win the love of Eugenia but even to have any authentic goals at all. Unlike the man in the second part of *Either/Or*, he does not overcome the distractions of an abundant thought-content, and he does not 'win through' to the state of an 'entirely individual human being'. He remains, rather, like the man in the first part of that book, whom Kierkegaard called 'an existential possibility which cannot win through to existence.... But the existential possibility ...keeps existence away by the most subtle of all deceptions, by thinking.'[35] Almost as soon as he meets her he makes it clear that the Eugenia with whom he is fascinated is herself almost

[35] *Unscientific Postscript*, p.227.

purely a product of his own thought: '¡Mi Eugenia, sí, la mía — iba diciéndose —, ésta que me estoy forjando a solas, y no la otra, no la de carne y hueso...' (ii, 561). As he comes actually to know the Eugenia 'de carne y hueso', she acquires an apparently greater reality for him than she has at this point, but the degree of that reality remains questionable.

For that matter everything, to be sure, is questionable for Augusto, and as we read his monologues it becomes clear that a large part of his thought consists of questions. There is really nothing in his experience which the compulsive doubter refrains from questioning: why does his servant Domingo have that name rather than another? (561); why does the mayor permit shops to use such ugly letters in their signs? (566). And ultimately, the total, metaphysical question: why should there be a God, or a world, or anything? (577). His questions take a great many different forms, but the question, why?, is the most typical, as well as often being the most widely encompassing. The Spanish form, *¿por qué?* is explicitly concerned with causes and origins, and it is therefore oriented toward the past, the previous reality which gave rise to present reality. As such it is in clear contrast to the *¿para qué?*, which is concerned with finalities and therefore with future reality. It is only after he has met Eugenia that the *¿para qué?* of life seems even to occur to Augusto, but even then the *¿por qué?* continues to dominate his thinking.

Ultimately this compulsive questioning must be seen as a symptom of a profound ontological insecurity, a radical doubt concerning the foundations of his own being. At one point he tells his friend Víctor that he has a 'manía de la introspección' which both fascinates and terrifies him, particularly when self-contemplation takes the literal form of gazing into a mirror (xxii, 635).[36] At other moments he has the feeling that his empirical self is a pure illusion, so that others literally do not see him, or that his empirical self is behaving in a way of which his conscious self is completely unaware (vii, 577).

[36] See also the comments on the mirror in the 'Introducción' to my edition of *Cómo se hace una novela* (Madrid: Guadarrama, 1977), pp.22-25. On the concept of the 'divided self', of which the fear of the mirror-image is one manifestation, see R.D. Laing, *The Divided Self* (Harmondsworth: Penguin, 1966).

A similar thought much later, after his last and completely unsuccessful encounter with Rosario, leads him to wonder if he is sane. He does, of course, suffer from the inner alienation of a profoundly divided self, and these fantasies are felt as possibilities and feared as dangers. They are, however, not hallucinations. The internal duality suggests that Augusto is a schizoid personality, but he is not schizophrenic. The alienation he suffers is not from outward reality but from his own inner feelings. Yet that internal alienation is a profound one, and his attempt to solve the problem of choosing between Rosario and Eugenia by undertaking a series of experiments in feminine psychology is only an intellectualization of a problem of conflicting desires, a conversion of its concrete realities into a series of abstractions which prevent, rather than enabling, confrontation with those realities.

There are a number of additional observations which remain to be made about the character of Augusto Pérez, but since most of them concern his relations with the other characters, I shall include them in my comments on each of them in turn. Just as the significance of Augusto's name was a useful starting-point for discussion of his entire role in the novel, that of the other characters' names proves to be equally useful in these comments.

Eugenia is the only character in the novel whose name is, in fact, the subject of some commentary in the novel itself. When Augusto learns from the *portera* that Eugenia's surnames are Domingo del Arco, he asks if when given to a woman the first surname should not be Dominga, pedantically adding, 'Y si no, ¿dónde está la concordancia?' (i, 558). Later he is about to decide to change her surname to Dominga, but then realizes that the problem of grammatical agreement will only return when they have male children who bear the second surname Dominga. The question of sexual identity and of the differences between the sexes cannot, he finds, be reduced to questions of grammatical gender.

Yet the form of her surname doubtless is significant. Feal Deibe suggests that it implies a basic androgyny (*17*, p.74) in her character, and this seems to be borne out in her attitudes and actions, if we assume that her capacity for cruelty, her aggressive self-assertiveness, and her aesthetic insensitivity (she loathes music, even though she teaches piano) are masculine traits. In addition to the gender of the surname, however, is the fact that it bears a very evident relation to such words as Latin *dominus* and Spanish *dominar*. The second surname further reinforces this by evoking the image of a triumphal arch. As for her given name, the literal meaning is 'well born' or 'noble', so that taken all together her name suggests — with none of the ambiguity in that of Augusto Pérez — that she is the august ruler. In another sense, the meaning 'well born' suggests the fact that she is 'thoroughly born' — that is, a full formed individual, who has completely differentiated herself from her origins and from dependence on others. These are, of course, the qualities in her which he most admires. When she angrily breaks off their first conversation after learning that he has been told about the mortgage on her house, he exclaims, '¡Si esta recia independencia de carácter, a mí, que no lo tengo, es lo que más me entusiasma!' (viii, 581-82).

What first attracted Augusto to her, of course, were her eyes, of which we are told nothing more than that they shine like stars — 'estrellas mellizas' whose light pierces through the mist (iii, 563-64). The only reference to other aspects of her appearance, as well as her eyes, occurs when they are being introduced: 'Los ojos de Eugenia, en un rostro todo frescor de vida y sobre un cuerpo que no parecía pesar sobre el suelo, dieron como una nueva luz espiritual a la escena' (viii, 580). As a description this is still very non-specific and abstract, but when he extends his hand at the actual moment of introduction, two specific physical details finally do occur: 'Una mano blanca y fría, blanca como la nieve y como la nieve fría, tocó su mano' (viii, 580).

The coldness of her hand is, of course, symbolic of the coldness with which she treats Augusto, and also of the coldness with which she calculates the realization of her own self-interest, her independence from others, and her urge to dominate. The first time she had noticed Augusto on the street, before their introduction, Eugenia reacted with a certain interest, saying to herself, '¿Quién será este joven? No tiene mal porte y parece bien acomodado!' (ii, 562), which suggests that the possibility of becoming interested in someone more well to do than her present fiancé is not offensive to her. Her reaction against having Augusto's suit supported by her aunt is very strong, however, and she clearly resents anything that might seem to compromise her independence, whether it be family pressures or Augusto's wealth itself. Later she comes to feel contempt for what she sees as his weakness of character, calling him a 'pobre panoli que vive en Babia' (ix, 584), and says that he is 'para mí como si no existiera... Si es hueco, como si lo viera, hueco' (xv, 605).

Nevertheless her sense of self-interest eventually leads her to overcome this repugnance to accept the gift of the mortgage on her house. This occurs after her break with her *novio*, Mauricio, who had refused either to find work so they could be married, or marry and allow Eugenia to continue working. For her part that alternative would have actually had certain advantages, since in that way, says Eugenia, Mauricio 'será mío, mío, y cuanto más de mí dependa, más mío' (xv, 608), but his own pride, or concern for the opinion of others, will not allow him to accept that solution.

Yet he is equally opposed to the idea of working himself in order to support Eugenia, and he has little reluctance in telling her that the best solution will be to marry Augusto but continue to have relations with him, her former *novio*. Mauricio's surnames are Blanco Clará, and since his given name is etymologically related to a Latin word meaning 'black', the entire name suggests that he sees everything in terms of black and white, avoiding all nebulous ambiguities in expressing his desires, no matter how indelicate they may appear. Eugenia's break with Mauricio at this point seems to be due to her belief that his suggestion is indecent, yet her subsequent actions indicate that her moral sensibilities are scarcely any more delicate than Mauricio's. She first lets Augusto know that she has decided to make the sacrifice of accepting his gift of the mortgage on her property, and then uses the very fact of having accepted his money as a means of enticing him into renewing his proposal of marriage, telling him in effect that people will naturally believe the gift means she has become his lover, and that therefore no one else will ever propose marriage to her.

It is true that there is some delay in his actually making the proposal, because their conversation is interrupted when the arrival of Rosario is announced by Liduvina, and since he finds himself more and more attracted by the laundry girl, he is faced by a dilemma which he tries to resolve through the psychological experiments undertaken at the suggestion of Antolín S. Paparrigópulos. After the failure of his attempt to experience sexual love with Rosario, he turns to Eugenia with the intention of experimenting to see if she will accept a proposal of marriage. He both suspects that she has been planning all along to get him to do precisely this, and seems convinced that she will never accept him, but she does, in fact, accept his proposal, letting him know that it is neither out of gratitude for his generosity nor from anger for what happened to her with Mauricio (xxvi, 651), but out of pity for him, and in order to save him from women like Rosario.

This makes it quite clear that part of her motive for accepting Augusto is simple jealousy. As soon as she had heard from doña Ermelinda of his somewhat haughty response to the news that she had decided to accept his gift, she became convinced there was another woman in his life and declared her intention of winning him again (xix, 623). It is also quite probable that her decision to break the engagement to Augusto a few days before their wedding in order to go with Mauricio to the town in which he will take up the position Augusto has obtained for him is motivated in part by jealousy when she learns that Rosario is to accompany Mauricio. We are never told directly that she has heard of it, but her manner of asking Augusto what has happened to Rosario makes him certain that she knows of it. It is possible, of course, that she also prefers Mauricio as a man, since the contempt she had expressed for Augusto on account of his self-sacrificing generosity does not really seem to have been put aside, but jealousy is clearly a major motive for her actions.

Perhaps her principal motive, however, is to be found in the will to dominate implied by her name. By marrying a man who has a job which she obtained for him through Augusto, she has a husband who is much more dependent on her than if she married one who is independently wealthy. We are never told specifically that she and Mauricio plan to marry, but on the assumption that Eugenia would thereby assure her dominance over Mauricio we may reasonably conclude that they do. There is little to indicate that any other concern — except, of course, a prudent consideration of public opinion — would have been very significant in her thinking. In her note to Augusto she mentions that 'Mauricio quería que nos hubiéramos escapado el día mismo de la boda, después de salir de la iglesia; pero su plan era muy complicado y me pareció, además, una crueldad inútil' (xxix, 659). Clearly, then, Mauricio proposed — and Eugenia at least briefly considered — her going through with the wedding and running away immediately upon leaving the church. Her rejection of it is not due to its immorality but simply because, in the first place, the plan was too complicated, and only secondly because it was a 'crueldad inútil'. It if had been a useful cruelty, she apparently would have had no objection to it whatever.

Quite the opposite of the cruelty, selfishness, and cool superiority of Eugenia are the humility, generosity, and submissiveness of the laundry-girl, Rosario. We are told very little about her appearance except that she has a beauty which Augusto finally notices after his fascination with Eugenia has opened his eyes to the attractions of all women. Her name recalls, of course, a specific practice of devotion to the Virgin, but it also retains a number of natural, archetypal associations, particularly with feminine sexuality.[37] When she first appears with Augusto's freshly pressed clothing he stares at her intently enough to make her blush, despite the fact that she is accustomed to being stared at with obvious desire by other men. When he tells her to come over to him, she rises as if under hypnotic suggestion and allows him to take her on his lap. He asks if she will love him, and she compliantly responds: 'Creo que sí..., que le querré...' (xii, 596).

In their next conversation he tells her to forget what happened the previous time, and she answers, 'Bueno, como usted

[37] These archetypal associations are, of course, more specifically related to the image of the individual rose, but surely the name implies that image as well as that of a rose garden. See J.E. Cirlot, *A Dictionary of Symbols* (New York: Philosophical Library, 1962) for entries under 'Rose', 'Flower', and 'Garden'.

quiera...' (xviii, 617), but immediately thereafter he again takes her on his lap. The contradiction seems not to disturb her in the least, but when he questions her about her relations with other young men she again bursts into tears. He then tells her that the other woman has just rejected him completely and that he plans to take a long journey. He asks if she will go with him, and again she replies, characteristically, 'Como usted quiera...' He then begins to kiss her, fervently, perhaps, rather than passionately, and her acceptance of Augusto is so complete as to suggest she would not even refuse the greatest intimacy at this point. Yet he seems to feel some obstacle to the realization of his own desires, and he suddenly rises and says, '¡Déjame! ¡Déjame! ¡Tengo miedo!' (xviii, 618). After she leaves he engages in some reflections which prove to be of great thematic significance: 'La he estado mintiendo y he estado mintiéndome... El hombre en cuanto habla miente... No hay más verdad que la vida fisio-lógica ...' (xviii, 619).

Eventually he puts physiological truth to the test when Rosario comes to see him just as he is planning to undertake his series of experiments in feminine psychology. He had planned to begin with Eugenia, pretending again to seek her hand, but when Rosario arrives he almost immediately takes her again on his lap. At first he is somewhat confused, but he soon embraces and kisses her warmly. He then picks her up and puts her on the sofa, but all he does is stare into her eyes, saying, '¡No los cierres, Rosario, no los cierres, por Dios! ...Déjame que me vea en ellos, tan chiquitito...' (xxiv, 645). At this point, we are told, he felt his first excitement abating. He asks her to forgive him, because he did not know what he was doing, but her thought is, 'Lo que no se sabe es lo que no se hace' (xxiv, 646), and she leaves convinced that he is dangerously mad.

He feels quite ridiculous over the incident and asks himself what Rosario could have thought of him. He concludes, however, that it really does not matter what she thinks: 'Es un ser fisiológico, perfectamente fisiológico..., sin psicología alguna' (xxiv, 647). At best, therefore, she could only be taken as a subject for physiological or psycho-physiological experiments (which is what he has presumably just been engaged in), but the study of psycho-physiology requires technical training and the appropriate apparatus. With a touch of sadness he acknowledges that 'carezco...de aparatos' (xxiv, 647), which the last scene with Rosario shows to have been all too true.

When Mauricio comes to see Augusto some time later, ostensibly to thank him for having found him a position, but actually to enjoy Augusto's discomfiture when he lets him know he is now intimate with Rosario, Augusto becomes so angry that he lifts Mauricio up and throws him on the sofa as if to strangle him. Perhaps this is not too improbable a way of making a murderous attack, but it is made highly ambiguous by the many parallels between this scene and the one with Rosario, which the narrator is careful to emphasize: the same room, the same action (described by the same expression, 'levantar en vilo'), and the same sofa. And Mauricio ironically adds another parallel by saying, 'Mírese usted ahora, don Augusto, en mis pupilas y verá qué chiquitito se ve' (xviii, 656), whereupon Augusto's passionate anger passes. These parallels do not, I think, imply that Augusto is actually directing a disguised eroticism toward his rival, but only that he sees in him the success in amorous affairs which he desires for himself and furiously tries to seize by attacking him.

The last mention of Rosario in the novel occurs just before Eugenia leaves Augusto for Mauricio. Since learning that Rosario was going away with his rival, Augusto has felt terrible jealousy of him, as well as anger with himself for letting pass the opportunity he had had with the girl, and for the ridiculous role he has played with her. Apparently he believes his failure to consummate his love with Rosario was purely voluntary on his part, for we are told he even thinks of changing his mind about the two women (xxix, 658). So greatly does jealousy alter his esteem for them that he even imagines Mauricio laughing at him precisely because of having been able to foist Eugenia off on him and get the more lovable and loving Rosario for himself.

A number of critics have suggested that the reason for Augusto's problems in love is his profound and abiding attachment to his mother, which makes him unconsciously avoid mature sexual love and constantly seek a relationship of child-like dependency on a maternal figure.[38] The frequency with which he invokes her memory, precisely when he has been thinking about Eugenia, is one of a number of indications that this is precisely the problem. It even seems likely that his fixation on a woman as cold and inherently unattainable as Eugenia was in itself a means of avoiding authentic relationships with women by entering one which in retrospect, at least, was from the start virtually certain to be doomed to failure. The name of Augusto's mother, like that of the other principal characters, is no doubt intentionally significant. She is referred to simply as doña Soledad, which expresses both the near solitude in which she is left as a widow and the fact that before her death she was the sole and unique woman — almost, in fact, the sole being — in Augusto's life. The description of their life together suggests a relationship which was nearly symbiotic. What he did not want to eat at meals she did not eat either. She was the first thing he saw every morning, and she never went to bed before he did, so that he was never able to *trasnochar*. She studied his lessons with him and drilled him in them, so that she even shared his intellectual life. She may also have had an influence in the problem he has with the physiological aspect of life and love, because we are told Physiology was the one subject for which she showed no enthusiasm (v, 572).

Among the secondary characters of *Niebla*, Augusto's cook, Liduvina, is in one sense probably the most important, if only because she becomes part of the developmental structure in the novel's theoretical sub-text which I discussed in Chapter 2. She is also the one character whose physical description includes at least a few precise details, so that she is the one of whom we have the fullest sense of a physical presence. Like her husband, Domingo, she has a great deal of the common sense of the lower classes. When Augusto first mentions the possibility of marrying she expresses caution, saying that the advisability of it is 'según y conforme' (iv, 567) — depending, that is, on whom he marries. It is also she who reminds him of his mother's advice to marry a woman who will love and govern him. Her name is one which

---

[38] Those who have emphasized this analysis of his behavior most explicitly are Feal Deibe (*17*) and Gullón (*19*).

Unamuno tells us in the prologue to *San Manuel Bueno y tres historias más* is common in the country around Salamanca. He says it interested him especially because popular etymology has often changed it to Luzdivina, which, given her role as a surrogate mother to Augusto, may be significant with respect to his attachment to his mother and continuing search for maternal figures.[39]

Víctor Goti is certainly a character of major importance in the novel, although not in the sense of active involvement in the events of the plot. As author of the prologue, narrator of his own interpolated tale, and frequent confidant of Augusto, he pervades the entire novel, not as a spiritual presence like that of Augusto's departed mother, but as an intellectual and critical perspective. To a great extent that function is, of course, an authorial one, and he can even be personally identified with Unamuno to some extent, since the surname Goti is that of a *quinto abuelo* of the author himself. Víctor's given name may be seen as implying that having solved his own problems with respect to marriage and family life, he has been able, in the phrase I have quoted from Kierkegaard, to 'win through to existence'. It is also possible that the name deliberately echoes that of Kierkegaard's Victor Eremita in *Either/Or*, in which he appears as the fictional editor and author of a prologue.[40]

In the role of interlocutor and confidant to Augusto Pérez, Víctor Goti's attitudes are completely devoid of sentimentality and come very close to lacking in sympathy as well. When Augusto first tells him he is in love, Víctor's comment dismisses his friend's feelings as a mere 'amorío innato' (iii, 565). Later he tells him that his love is purely cerebral, 'de cabeza', and even goes on to say, '—Y si me apuras mucho te digo que tú mismo no eres sino una pura idea, un ente de ficción' (x, 589), which Augusto finds deeply offensive to his ego because he takes it to

[39] It is worth noting that Augusto's fascination with Eugenia's eyes also leads him to emphasize the fact that they are a kind of divine light.

[40] This suggestion concerning a possible influence from Kierkegaard, like those presented in Webber's study and elsewhere, is based on the evidence of Unamuno's thorough knowledge of the Danish philosopher's work offered by the abundant markings and marginal notes in his own set of the collected works of Kierkegaard in Danish. Concerning Unamuno's ancestor, don Pedro Goti, see Ribbans (*24*, 109).

imply he is incapable of really falling in love as other men do. His calling Augusto an 'ente de ficción' seems at this point to be a mere intellectual conceit, but it does, of course, anticipate Unamuno's words at the end of the novel and it is therefore a further indication of his basic identity with the author.

Perhaps the statement which reveals most about Víctor is his advice to Augusto during their final conversation to 'devour himself', confusing the pleasure of devouring with the pain of being devoured. In that way, he tells him, 'llegarás a la perfecta ecuanimidad de espíritu, a la ataraxia; no serás sino un mero espectáculo para ti mismo' (xxx, 662). His advice for relieving emotional suffering is, then, to separate thought from feeling, distancing the affective self from the intellectual self and intellectualizing sentiment — which is virtually the same as repressing it altogether. Augusto regards this advice as equivalent to suggesting that he commit suicide, and Víctor does not deny this may be so: '—No digo ni que sí ni que no. Sería una solución como otra, pero no la mejor' (xxx, 661). His whole manner of thinking, then, is literally 'corrosiva', as Augusto calls it (xxx, 662), at the same time that it deliberately tends toward confusion: 'Y hay que confundir... Confundir el sueño con la vela, la ficción con la realidad, lo verdadero con lo falso; confundirlo todo en una sola niebla' (xxx, 661). This, too, is a reflection of Unamuno himself, since Goti's prologue had quoted the author as affirming that 'lo mío es indefinir, confundir' (Prólogo, 545). [41]

Another figure who serves chiefly as an interlocutor for Augusto is Antolín S. Paparrigópulos, whom he consults about his interest in feminine psychology. López-Morillas has pointed out his similarity to satirical figures in the earlier novels, such as the poet Hildebrando F. Menaguti in *Amor y pedagogía*, and the young Carlist intellectual in *Paz en la guerra* (*21*). A similar figure, named Joaquín Rodríguez Janssen, also appears in a satire published in *Revista Nueva* in 1899 (Ribbans, *24*, 103). All

---

[41] In Goti's prologue this comment is related to the statement attributed to Unamuno that it is his ambition to write a work which will be a true fusion — not merely a mixture — of the farcical and the tragic, an ambition which most readers agree has been more fully realized in *Niebla* than in any other work in our century, with the possible exception of certain works of Joyce and Kafka.

of them satirize the kind of erudition represented by Marcelino Menéndez y Pelayo, the Catholic intellectual whose precocious display of learning had won acclaim in conservative circles, while Unamuno and other liberals regarded it as pretentious pedantry. According to López-Morillas, the completely self-satisfied Paparrigópulos is an extreme example of the kind of character he calls an *antagonista*, whose struggles are purely with the external world, in contrast to the *agonista*, whose struggles are mainly within (*21*, 11-39). The critic regards the former as a product of the premeditated literary creation of the *escritor ovíparo*, more typical in Unamuno's early works, while the latter is created by the *escritor vivíparo* and comes to predominate in the later works.

The significance of the name of Paparrigópulos is not to be found in its literal meaning (as a modern Greek patronymic, it simply means 'son of Father Rigos') but in its structure, which combines a Spanish given name and paternal surname with a foreign maternal surname and then reduces the paternal one to an initial. The choice of Paparrigópulos for the maternal surname is probably mostly for the purpose of having one which would sound comically outlandish to Spanish ears, but being longer and more sonorous than Sánchez (especially when reduced to S.), it suggests that for all his pretensions to being supremely *castizo* and thoroughly masculine in his thinking, the foreign and the feminine elements actually predominate in him. Augusto's visit to him almost constitutes another interpolated tale in the novel, but he really has no story of his own beyond that which is implied in the description of his ideas by the narrator. His principal function is thematic, but it is also important to note that it is he who precipitates Augusto's actions, leading the novel to its climax.

Much more involved with the entire action of the novel, however, are Eugenia's aunt and uncle, doña Ermelinda Ruiz y Ruiz, and don Fermín. Feal Deibe suggests that her name, like that of Eugenia Domingo del Arco, implies an androgynous personality, interpreting the given name as 'Hermes-linda', and the identity of the two *apellidos* as implying the complete assimilation of the masculine to the feminine (*17*, p.83). In general this inteptetation seems plausible, since it is true that doña Ermelinda completely dominates her husband. It is also she who takes an active role in proposing to Eugenia that she accept Augusto as a suitor. The name of don Fermín is, of course, a perfectly normal one, but since so many other characters have symbolic names, it seems quite natural that we should relate his name to forms like *enfermo/enfermín* (i.e., *enfermizo*) when we recall the many times Unamuno has spoken of reason, intelligence, and consciousness itself as being deleterious to life and as a kind of illness.[42] Don Fermín is a pure intellectual, espousing a complex of ideas constituting a kind of 'anarquismo espiritual' which seeks to reform society, marriage, language, and even Spanish orthography. His one practical comment is given to Augusto in an aside, since it contradicts his wife's encouragement of Augusto's hope of winning Eugenia: 'Al salir se le acercó un momento don Fermín y le dijo al oído: "No piense usted en eso!" "¿Y por qué no?" —le preguntó Augusto—. "¡Hay presentimientos, caballero, hay presentimientos...!"' (vi, 576). The exact nature of his presentiments is never made clear, but they may well be related to his experience of living with a domineering wife.

Also to be included in any survey of the characters of *Niebla* is, of course, the author himself, who appears first simply as an authorial voice in the final paragraph of Chapter XXV, commenting on what he has just seen and heard in the conversation between Augusto and Víctor in the preceding part of the chapter. At this stage he is only a short distance away from the presumably impersonal, third-person narrator who has told the whole story up to that point, but the introduction of the

[42] In *En torno al casticismo*, for example, Unamuno warns that a hypertrophied consciousness causes inner life to languish (I, 867), and in the 'Oración fúnebre' in *Niebla* itself Orfeo expresses the idea that man 'es un animal enfermo, no cabe duda... ¡Sólo parece gozar de alguna salud cuando duerme...!' (Epílogo, 680). With respect to the name of Ermelinda, although I find Feal Deibe's interpretation fairly plausible, it should also be pointed out that it is a near anagram of that of doña Edelmira, the wife of the philosopher, don Fulgencio, in *Amor y pedagogía*. The similarity of the women (and their husbands) in the two novels tends to corroborate Ribbans's view of *Niebla* as being very nearly a revised version of the earlier novel. At the same time, the similarity of their names suggests that there is in both of them a kind of undifferentiated feminine substance, which is always the same.

author's *yo* drastically alters the character of the entire text, revealing the very personal perspective which had always been present beneath the masque of impersonality: '*Mientras Augusto y Víctor sostenían esta conversación* nivolesca, *yo, el autor de esta* nivola, *que tienes, lector, en la mano y estás leyendo, me sonreía enigmáticamente al ver que mis* nivolescos *personajes estaban abogando por mí y justificando mis procedimientos...*' (xxv, 649). He then compares this to the manner in which men justify the ways of God whenever they seek to justify themselves, and declares himself to be the god who has created these two characters.

The whole interpolation is a reminder that the characters are purely fictional creations of the author, but by presenting himself as observer and eavesdropper on the conversation he nevertheless reinforces the idea that they are, at the same time, autonomous characters, who speak not as the author dictates but in accord with their own impulses. A much greater step away from the perspective of the impersonal narrator is taken in the chapter (xxxi) presenting the conversation between Augusto and his author, but the basic paradox remains. On the one hand the fictionality of the character is emphasized by the author who tells him he cannot commit suicide because he, the author, does not feel like permitting it (xxxi, 667). On the other hand, the very fact of engaging in discussion with his character implies, as Augusto himself points out, a recognition of existence which is independent from his author.

The Unamuno who engages in discussion with Augusto Pérez, like the one who overheard the conversation between Augusto and Víctor, maintains a complacently superior attitude toward his characters, smiling enigmatically at their ignorance concerning their true condition, addressing Augusto with an authoritarian *tú*, becoming indignant when the character then questions his own real existence, and furious when he insinuates that he might kill his author rather than himself. He then decrees Augusto's death in the most extravagant juridical language: 'Y para castigar tu osadía y esas doctrinas disolventes, extravagantes, anárquicas, con que me has venido, resuelvo y fallo que te mueras' (xxxi, 669), and when Augusto fervently pleads for his life, Unamuno is implacable.

This Unamuno the author/character is, then, one who has fairly conventional ideas as to the extent of his power over his characters and concerning the difference between the mode of being of fictional characters and real persons. The only respects in which he seems unconventional are in his failure to be surprised at having his character come to see him, and, perhaps, in his idea that Augusto is a product not only of his own fantasy but of that of his readers also. After Augusto's death he adopts a much milder attitude toward him and even decides to revive him and allow him to commit suicide if that is his wish. When Augusto comes to him in a dream, however, he tells him it would be impossible, and Unamuno is immediately persuaded by everything Augusto says. Even when Unamuno asks if he might again dream him, Augusto answers, echoing Heraclitus: 'No se sueña dos veces el mismo sueño' (xxxiii, 678),[43] which the author completely accepts, and when his character repeats the warning that it might, in fact, be Unamuno who is the fictional being, there is no reaction of indignation whatever. By now it is clear that the author/character has become much less sure of himself, and much less certain that fiction and reality are profoundly and radically distinct.

The last of the characters who must be included in this survey is Augusto's dog, Orfeo, which he had found abandoned as a new-born pup among some bushes of the Alameda (v). It is clear that Augusto feels a great sympathy for the dog, and even identifies with him to a considerable extent. When the servant Domingo refers to the animal as *expósito*, Augusto's immediate comment is: '—Todos somos expósitos, Domingo' (v, 573), and in a number of other ways it is clear that he feels as though he and the dog are fellow castaways.

As soon as he brings the dog home Augusto gives him the name Orfeo, about which the narrator says, 'así le bautizó, no se sabe ni sabía él tampoco por qué' (v, 573). This would seem to discourage any effort to look for any meaning in the name, but at the same time it implies that it would be normal for there to be

[43] I refer, of course, to the famous maxim of Heraclitus in his Fragment 91: 'It is not possible to step twice into the same river.'

a particular motive in the name. Feal Deibe relates it to the myth
of Orpheus, suggesting a parallel between love and fidelity of the
dog for Augusto and of Orpheus for Eurydice, which inspires
both Orfeos to follow the object of love into the realm of death
(*17*, p.121). Certainly that parallel exists, but since Orpheus
returns, while Orfeo does not, the analogy is clearly a very
limited one. It is, in any case, a very ironic parallel, very much in
keeping with the irony of the entire novel, and it must be
admitted that the divergence is entirely in accord with
Unamuno's own belief that there is no return from death. One
other possible dimension of meaning in Orfeo's name might,
perhaps, be found in the phonetic similarity between *Orfeo* and
huérfano, the meaning of which is, of course, very similar to
that of *expósito*. The narrator tells us that after Augusto's
death, 'Orfeo, en efecto, quedó huérfano' (Epílogo, 679), a
sentence which seems to emphasize the similarity of sound, at
the same time that it reminds us of the abandonment with which
Orfeo — and Augusto — had both entered and left the world of
the novel.

Orfeo's principal function in the novel is that of silent listener
to Augusto's monologues, some of which, we are told, are silent
themselves. Parker has convincingly shown that he also
symbolizes the physiological and sensual aspects of life, and that
'whenever Augusto's introspection takes a concretely sensual, or
sexual, form the dog appears' (*32*, p.128). Orfeo's love is
completely spontaneous and sincere, precisely because it is
unmediated by language. When Augusto has been reflecting that
man always lies as soon as he speaks, he says to Orfeo, 'Tú como
no hablas no mientes, y hasta creo que no te equivocas, que no te
mientes' (xviii, 619). Finally, as Augusto himself emphasizes,
the dog symbolizes fidelity, which is what particularly disturbs
him when Eugenia insists that she will not have Orfeo in the
house after they are married (xxviii, 657).

Throughout the novel proper Orfeo's actions are purely those
of a normal dog in relation to his master, accepting the milk
Augusto offers him, occasionally licking his hand, and patiently
listening to his monologues while staring up at him with eyes
that seem to understand. So understanding does he seem,

however, that the monologues are almost dialogues, as Augusto asks him numerous questions — including such things as whether he has not had experiences similar to his own (vii, 577-78) — and at times even asking his advice (xxiii, 637). Only in the 'Oración fúnebre por modo de epílogo' do we have an articulate expression of thought by Orfeo, but it is presented purely as unspoken thought, which the narrator articulates for him. The 'Oración' echoes Augusto's belief that 'el hombre en cuanto habla miente' as Orfeo says of man that 'el lenguaje le ha hecho hipócrita' (Epílogo, 680). Beyond that it is a view of man, both sympathetic and cynical (both in the etymological sense of 'canine' and in the figurative sense of 'critical'), as an animal 'que habla, que se viste y que almacena sus muertos' (Epílogo, 681).

Summarizing Unamuno's technique of characterization in *Niebla*, one does, I believe, have to grant that his use of names which are symbolic or in some way significant, his grotesque exaggeration of some character traits for comical and satirical purposes, his occasional touches of ideological polemic (as in the *reductio ad absurdum* of the ideas of Paparrigópulos), and the complete absence of anything like physical portraits or description of physical settings in which they live, all tend to make the characters of *Niebla* quite different from those of the classic realist novel. There is very little illusion that these are persons of flesh and blood, whose history has been objectively recorded, even aside from the impossible situation of the conversation between author and character or of the eloquent dog. *Niebla* is very much a novel of ideas — ideas about language and literature, about the condition of man in the world and in time, about the mind/body problem, and about the metaphysical foundations of all of reality — which the characters represent and give expression to. In creating them Unamuno has been more concerned with truth than with literary realism. Particularly in the character of Augusto Pérez he has, I believe, succeeded in representing human life as a 'flujo vivo de contradicciones, como una serie de yos, como un río espiritual', as he expressed it in the passage quoted earlier in this chapter. Augusto's conception of human life as one in which 'caminamos

...por una selva enmarañada y bravía, sin senderos' and where 'el sendero nos lo hacemos con los pies según caminamos a la ventura' is fully in agreement with his author's belief in the essential fluidity of human life.[44]

In one sense the very lack of realism in the characters of *Niebla* is what most effectively makes us aware of their truthfulness and helps us perceive the reality of our condition and of their condition as literary entities. Their frequent comments on the nature of language remind us that their only reality is that of the linguistic structures that embody them. They are purely products of thought — that of the author as he writes and of the reader as he reads — or, more precisely, they are themselves purely thoughts. If Augusto's body seems to fail him at a critical moment in the course of his efforts to realize his own existence by achieving intimate knowledge of the real existence of another, we are free to speculate on the causes of his impotence in psycho-analytic terms if we choose, but the basic fact is that Augusto's body has failed him for the very simple reason that he never had one to begin with. In *Niebla* Unamuno reminds us of the very obvious fact that no literary character can ever emerge from the mist of insubstantial thought to enter the determinate reality of material existence.[45] At the same time, however, he reminds us of the much less obvious fact that the concept of material existence is itself — as concept — simply another entity of thought, and that it is therefore not nearly so easy as we usually think to distinguish between beings that are mere fictions and those that really exist.

Despite his emphasis, in works like *Del sentimiento trágico*, on the primacy of 'el hombre de carne y hueso', it is clear that for Unamuno what most distinguishes man from other living

[44] The image of the path which is made 'según caminamos' has reminded many readers of the famous verses of Antonio Machado: 'Caminante, son tus huellas / el camino, y nada más; / caminante, no hay camino, / se hace camino al andar...' (*Proverbios y cantares*, xxix). In both writers the image of life as *camino* echoes Dante's 'cammin di nostra vita', and Augusto's 'selva enmarañada y bravía' also recalls Dante's 'selva selvaggia e aspra e forte' (*Inferno* I, 1-5).

[45] In *En torno al casticismo* Unamuno defended himself against possible complaints that he was simply pointing out the obvious and the familiar by insisting: 'Hace mucha falta que se repita a diario lo que a diario *de puro sabido se olvida*' (I, 784).

beings is the fact that he is a creature of language, thought, and consciousness. Since the fictional character, too, is a creature of language, he is also, in a sense, a creature of thought, and comes very close to having consciousness as well. It is true that these are in the first instance those of the author in the act of writing and of the reader in the moment of reading, but there is one thing which is purely his own, inherent in the language of which he is a creature — that is, what Augusto calls his own 'lógica interna' (xxxi, 667-68). Such logic is itself a principle of unity and a principle of continuity, which are what Unamuno, in the passage quoted at the beginning of this Chapter, regarded as fundamental determinants of man. In this respect, too, the difference between characters of fiction and real human beings proves to be very slight.

4. The interpolated tales

The analysis of structure which I presented in Chapter 2 shows that the interpolated tales are all placed in the central section of the novel, thereby defining that section's formal limits and characterizing it as a period of reflection and reorientation in the life of the protagonist. It is true that this section also includes the novel's major reversal of relationships, in that it begins with Eugenia's coming to denounce Augusto for having bought her mortgage, which she sees as an effort to gain power over her (xiii), moves from there to her break with Mauricio in one of the middle chapters (xvi), and ends soon after she has again visited Augusto, this time to accept his gift of the mortgage (xx). Nevertheless, Augusto himself is largely passive throughout the section, seeking guidance in matters of the heart by listening to a variety of narratives setting forth the experiences of others.

Early critics of *Niebla* tended to regard the interpolations negatively, as disruptive of the novel's unity of action, especially since they regarded them as being of such inherent triviality that they make no significant contribution to the novel itself.[46] More recently, however, such critics as Ribbans (*24*), Stevens (*33*), and Webber (*34*) have shown that their relevance to Augusto's problems makes them contribute very significantly to the thematic unity of the work. Finally, I believe my study of their placement within the central section shows that they give formal as well as thematic unity to the section, and at the same time articulate the general structure of the entire novel.

The incorporation of narratives within narratives is virtually as old as literature itself, but there is little doubt that the procedure here has been inspired by two quite specific models, *Don Quijote* and Kierkegaard's *Diary of a Seducer*. The first of

---

[46] Carlos Clavería, for example, calls them 'capítulos de chismografía de cualquier casino provinciano' (*Temas de Unamuno* (Madrid: Gredos, 1953), p.52). Julián Marías also speaks of them rather negatively, as 'mínimos mundos íntimos o de grotesca trivialidad' (*22*, p.99).

these influences might well have been simply assumed, even if no
mention were made of it in *Niebla*, but it becomes, in fact, very
explicit when Víctor Goti tells Augusto that he plans to
incorporate the story of Don Eloíno into a novel — that is, the
nivola — he is himself writing, 'como Cervantes metió en su
Quijote aquellas novelas que en él figuran' (xvii, 615). As for the
influence from Kierkegaard, Ruth House Webber convincingly
shows (*34*) how striking are the similarities between *Niebla* and
the *Diary* contained within *Either/Or*. Although the actual
content of the interpolations is quite different in the two works,
the fact that there are no fewer than eleven of them in the *Diary*
obviously determines significantly the general character of that
work, and since Unamuno was so clearly influenced by
numerous other aspects of it, this feature of its structure must
also have been very much in his mind.

Critical discussion of the interpolated tales varies somewhat in
terms of the number of episodes counted as tales, and also with
respect to which ones ought to be regarded purely as interpolations. Julián Marías believes there are six (*22*, p.98). Harriet
Stevens says there are five, including the Paparrigópulos
episode, but she adds Goti's own tale to her study (*33*, p.1),
again making six, although not the same as Marías's six.
Webber's list includes all those discussed by Stevens and adds
the one-paragraph anecdote told by Eugenia (xv, 607) for the
purpose of showing how brutish men are. Webber's count
therefore gives us seven such interpolations.

I believe, however, that the very short anecdotes ought not to
be regarded as interpolated tales, and I also exclude the
Paparrigópulos episode from the list of interpolations, precisely
because it is an integral part of the plot.[47] Therefore I shall here
discuss the five brief narratives which I believe can properly be
regarded as the interpolated tales of *Niebla*, all of which are in
some way exemplary of problems in love and marriage.

The first of these is the story of don Avito Carrascal, whom
Augusto meets in a church after a violent scene in which Eugenia

[47] Juan López-Morillas regards the introduction of Paparrigópulos as
aesthetically inopportune and very much as an anachronism, arguing
convincingly that the figure was conceived of a number of years earlier (*21*,
p.249: p.37 as reprinted in *Intelectuales y espirituales*).

expressed her anger over his purchase of her mortgage and her scorn both for him and the gift he tried to make of it. Don Avito had appeared in a central role in *Amor y pedagogía*, as a scientific rationalist who had decided to marry deductively — that is, deducing his choice of a wife and future mother of a son from scientific principles. This plan had as its goal the procreation and raising of a son who would be a genius, and therefore an example of what could be done to improve the human race by means of scientific pedagogy. From the very beginning, however, the plan has to be modified, as don Avito finds himself falling in love with a woman of different hair color and skull formation from those he had prescribed. He therefore marries inductively rather than deductively. Much of this is known to Augusto, who asks about the 'candidato a genio' (xiii, 599) and learns from don Avito's reply of the son's death by suicide. That event does not, however, constitute the interpolated tale itself, since all we learn of that reply in the text of *Niebla* is that don Avito 'le contó la lamentable historia de su hijo' (xiii, 599).

The story of his son is therefore an implicit tale within the tale of don Avito, whose story is one of disillusionment with scientific rationalism upon seeing its disastrous failure in the raising of his son. The immediate cause of the suicide was an unhappy love affair, but it is clear that the son has all along been a victim of his father's grim determination to make him distinguish himself as a genius of the purest rationality, with no provision made for more purely vital and emotional aspects of life. In the earlier novel don Avito had proclaimed: 'Sólo la ciencia es maestra de la vida' (II, 317); now he tells Augusto that 'la vida es la única maestra de la vida; no hay pedagogía que valga' (xiii, 599). What makes his story an exemplary one for Augusto is the fact that since the death of his son his wife has given him the maternal consolation he badly needs. He therefore tells Augusto that if he wants to have a mother again he should by all means marry. '—¿Y si la mujer a quien quiero no me quiere?', asks Augusto (xiii, 600), to which the immediate reply is: '—Cásate con la mujer que te quiera, aunque no la quieras tu.' At this point the image of Rosario comes to Augusto's mind, because 'se había hecho la ilusión de que aquella pobrecita quedó enamorada de él' (xiii, 600). The thought that she loves him may be an *ilusión* in the sense of 'illusion', or in the frequent Spanish sense of 'intriguing notion', but it seems clear that Rosario, unlike Eugenia, is at least able to love him, since she is basically a loving person. The moral to be learned from this exemplary tale is, then, a positive one: marriage is desirable if one can find a loving wife.

Víctor Goti's narrative of his own married life (xiv) may not, as Harriet Stevens seems to feel, be as purely an interpolation as most of the other narratives, since he is such a constantly recurring presence throughout almost the entire novel, but his story clearly has as much of an exemplary function for Augusto as any of the other tales, and in relation to the main plot it is also fully as marginal as the others. One day in the Casino Víctor tells Augusto that he and his wife had married very young, under pressure from both his and her parents, when they learned of an amorous episode which the two had had, almost by chance. Víctor says that it was, however, 'una falsa alarma' (xiv, 601), because the girl did not become pregnant, nor did she in the subsequent years of their marriage. Nevertheless they both very much wanted a child and eventually took to indulging in mutual recriminations and accusations of blame for their situation. Víctor frankly admits that it made him feel less worthy than other married men, and he began to eat voraciously of every-thing he believed to be most nutritious and aphrodisiac and to frequent his wife as much as possible, until he had a nervous collapse. After that they resigned themselves to childlessness and even to enjoy the advantages of a very well-ordered existence. Recently, however, his wife has become pregnant, and now they indulge in mutual blame for the new state of affairs and regard it as a 'mala jugada de la Providencia' (xiv, 603). They even refer to the unborn child as 'el intruso' and look forward to his birth with dread.

The moral of all this, drawn by Víctor for Augusto, is a completely sarcastic one: '—Conque ¡anda, Augusto, anda y cásate, para que acaso te suceda algo por el estilo; anda y cásate con la pianista!' (xiv, 604). Since 'algo por el estilo' seems to him so obviously undesirable, Víctor's 'cásate' is thoroughly ironic and actually means 'no te cases'. In another sense the story is also exemplary in showing the folly of wanting to have children merely out of vanity, of relying on merely popular notions as to how to increase potency and fertility, and of viewing sexual love in purely utilitarian terms, as a means toward the end of pro-creation.[48]

The portion of Víctor's married life presented thus far, and concluding with his ironic moral, is what I regard as actually constituting his interpolated story. It is true that it has a post-script when we learn (xxii) that a son has finally been born and everything has changed in their attitudes. Víctor will no longer permit the child to be called 'el intruso', and he finds his wife looking more beautiful than usual. There is, nevertheless, one negative aspect to fatherhood, which is that having children is what makes one old: 'Ver crecer al hijo es lo más dulce y lo más terrible, creo' (xxii, 636). He therefore tells Augusto not to marry if he wants the illusion of eternal youth. It is, however, ambiguous advice, since such an illusion does not really have much to recommend it, and he clearly thinks having children is the greatest joy. At this point, in any case, I believe we are dealing with an exchange of views which is part of the main narrative, rather than with an interpolated story like that which Víctor told in xiv.

The next interpolated tale is that of don Eloíno, an old bureaucrat of noble lineage who has married the owner of his *casa de huéspedes*. Víctor tells Augusto the grotesque circum-stances of this marriage in the course of their next conversation, in a chapter (xvii) which is almost at the exact center of the book. Don Eloíno had been moving from one boarding house to another in search of the greatest possible comfort for his paltry four pesetas a day, but no sooner had he found one than he became very gravely ill, and his landlady threatened to make him leave because caring for him was taking too much of her time. A friend therefore convinced him to ask the woman to marry him

[48] A counterpart and complement of the last of these morals, however, is a warning against settling into a routine of convenience and sexual gratification in marriage, to such an extent that one becomes nearly incapable of rising above petty self-interest.

and agree to let him stay there until his death, after which she would receive a widow's pension of 13 duros a month. When he has a brief recovery after the marriage, she accuses him of deceiving her and ends up making him leave after all. After his death she receives the pension and 500 pesetas for mourning attire, which she naturally spends on other things.

The exemplarity of this story for Augusto is to be found, of course, in showing the consequences of marrying purely for selfish reasons, whether they be those of don Eloíno in wanting to be cared for or those of doña Sinfo in marrying for the pension. The case is a clear warning against marrying Eugenia, who would do it only to gain control of Augusto's money, but it also suggests that a man's marrying in order to be cared for — implied by Augusto's search for a mother figure — is also unworthy and likely to have dire consequences. For Víctor it also seems to be exemplary purely as narrative also, since he plans to incorporate it as an interpolation in the novel — later called the *nivola* — he is writing. It is so grotesque that as an episode — presumably of real life — it has the quality of an interpolation of the fantastic into normal experience. It is therefore an exemplary interpolation, as well as an exemplary tale.

The story of don Antonio is the only one which occupies an entire chapter (xxi), so that no events of the main plot nor commentary on other important themes (such as Víctor's discussion of the *nivola* in the second part of xvii) can be found in addition to the tale itself. This makes it in structural terms the most readily dispensable of the chapters and the most purely interpolated of the stories, but the fact that it is nevertheless present tends to confirm what I have suggested about the structural importance in *Niebla* of the principle of symmetry, which would be destroyed if an interpolated tale did not appear precisely at this point. It does, of course, have an important exemplary function as well: don Antonio had married a woman with whom he was madly in love, but one day she ran off with another man who abandoned a wife and child, taking her money with him. Antonio then sought her out and offered to make her his housekeeper, in a new house and in a different city. Eventually — after learning that his legal wife has had a child by the other man — Antonio and the housekeeper begin to live as husband and wife and finally have four children of their own, even though the primary sentiments which join them seem to be only those of sorrow and jealousy. Don Antonio implies that he told this woman he loved her only once in all their years together. The description of the legal wife reminds one in some ways of the coldness of Eugenia, and the exemplarity of the tale is a clear warning as to what would happen if Augusto married Eugenia, even if he were later to find consolation in Rosario.

The last interpolated tale is that of the *fogueteiro*, the Portuguese fireworks-maker who was extremely proud of his wife's uncommon beauty. When an accidental explosion disfigured her face, he was left blind and completely unable to see the change in her, so he continued to boast of her beauty to others, who out of pity continued to praise her for it. This tale is told to Víctor by Augusto (xxii), who recalls it when Víctor tells him that since giving birth his wife seems more beautiful to him than ever, even though others tell him she seems to have aged at least ten years. Víctor's experience seems to confirm the traditional adage that love is blind, but the exemplarity of the *fogueteiro*'s case implies that blindness is actually an aid to love, and that beauty is in the mind — more than in the eye — of the beholder. Tragic as this story is, however, what it says about love in marriage is essentially favorable.

In this respect we may, in fact, see a kind of symmetrical progression in the series of five stories with respect to the relative favorableness of the views of love and marriage presented in them. The first (don Avito) and last (*fogueteiro*) are stories in which real tragedies occur, but love between the spouses is strong enough to bring consolation for the sorrow. In the second and fourth stories relations between the spouses are essentially positive, but shot through with ambiguity — because of the mutual recriminations between Víctor and his wife and the persistent sorrow, anger, and jealousy toward their former spouses in the case of don Antonio and his second wife. The central tale, that of don Eloíno, is the one giving the most negative view of the range of possibilities in marriage within the whole group. Here love is not merely ambiguous but totally lacking, and the effect in the marriage is grotesque. At the same time, however, the very fact that it is an extreme case perhaps makes it clear that in none of them is love free of egotism, whether it be that of don Avito in seeking maternal solicitude from his wife or of the *fogueteiro* in boasting of his wife's beauty. Taken all together the stories demonstrate that marriage is never free of ambiguity of feeling, or of difficulty and even tragedy. The most negative case (don Eloíno) is clearly an example to be avoided altogether, and if the following stories had not given more favorable examples, Augusto might have been persuaded to avoid marriage completely. The alternative, however, is to remain in a comfortable solitude which avoids complications but also avoids entering into the reality of existence — the reality of human life itself.

5. Theory and practice of the 'nivola'

In most editions of *Niebla* the term *nivola* is first encountered on the title-page, where it appears in parentheses, as if the unfamiliar word were an explanation for the more familiar one.[49] This paradox proves to be only the first of a great many with which the word is associated. Unfamiliar as it is to first-time readers of the novel, they may well get at least a general idea of its meaning, since its form and use suggest that it is somehow similar to *novela*, although no explanation of the word is given before the end of the middle chapter (xvii) of the book. It is there used by Víctor Goti, apparently as a spontaneously invented name for the kind of novel he is writing to distract himself from the irritation he feels because of his wife's pregnancy.

Víctor's comments on his novel occur just as he has finished telling Augusto the story of don Eloíno, when he remarks that he plans to incorporate it, 'de cualquier manera' (xvii, 615), into the novel he is writing. That phrase suggests from the very beginning that he conceives of the act of writing as something done quite spontaneously, and it becomes even clearer in his reply to a question from Augusto concerning the 'argumento' of his novel. Víctor says that his novel does not have one, or rather, that it will have the one that develops in the course of writing: 'El argumento se hace él solo.' He then describes how he came to start writing: 'Me senté, cojí unas cuartillas y empecé lo primero que se me ocurrió sin saber lo que seguiría, sin plan alguno. Mis personajes se irán haciendo según obren y hablen, sobre todo según hablen' (xvii, 615).

The passage clearly echoes what Unamuno had written in the essay, *A lo que salga* (see Chapter 1, n.8), concerning what he called the 'escritor vivíparo', who writes 'sin plan previo, y dejando que el plan surja' (I, 1195).

[49] The only exception, I believe, is the edition of Mario J. Valdés (*8*).

He then goes on to describe the difference between this method of writing and that of what he calls the 'escritor ovíparo', who, he says, 'Hace un esquema, plano o minuta de su obra, y trabaja luego sobre él; es decir, pone un huevo y lo empolla' (I, 1195). As for his own method of composition, Unamuno tells us that after writing *Paz en la guerra* by the oviparous method he underwent a profound change, so that '... me he lanzado a ejercitarme en el procedimiento vivíparo, y me pongo a escribir, como ahora he hecho, a lo que salga, aunque guiado, ¡claro está!, por una idea inicial...' (I, 1197).

Critics of *Niebla* have in any case long recognized that Unamuno may well have intended to create the effect of viviparous composition in the novel, but careful reading shows that it does, in fact, have a fairly complex 'plan previo'. The thematic coherence and exemplary appropriateness of the interpolated tales, as well as their symmetrical arrangement around the mid-point in the novel, shows that they are not introduced simply 'de cualquier manera', in the way that Víctor said he planned to incorporate the story of don Eloíno into his own novel. Other significant examples of symmetrical ordering, as in the sequence of the stages through which Augusto first advances and then regresses in his relations with women, are further evidence of careful planning.

I must therefore agree with critics who deny that the method of composition described in *A lo que salga* and in Víctor's discussion of his novel was followed in *Niebla* itself. As Ruth House Webber expresses this view: 'That this was the effect Unamuno intended to create and that he was eminently successful in creating it is undeniable, but that this was the process of composition is quite a different matter' (*34*, p.130). A large part of the novel's success in creating this effect is probably due to the character of Augusto Pérez himself. Because of his lack of determinate goals in life it is he who seems to 'caminar sin plan previo', as Unamuno had said of the method of writing 'a lo que salga'. When Augusto appears at the beginning of *Niebla* to go out for a walk he has no idea which direction to take and first decides to let it be determined simply by the direction taken by the first passing dog. When instead he follows 'una garrida moza' (i, 557) rather than a dog, it is as much without deliberate choice on his part as if he had let the direction be determined by a whim of chance, and he is completely unconscious of being drawn by the attraction of her eyes until she finally enters her house.

The free association of his thoughts as he unconsciously follows her produces one of the most remarkable passages of the stream-of-consciousness technique in the modern novel (i, 557-58), in which the series of objective experiences and chance encounters he has in the course of his walk — the child staring at an ant on the ground, the man elbowing his way through the crowd, the chocolate maker wielding his pestle in a shop window, the paralyzed beggar, a friend named Joaquín, a passing automobile, and finally some problem with his umbrella — could all be characterized in the terms used in the first of the passages here quoted from *A lo que salga*. It would be entirely apt to say that Augusto is walking 'sin saber adónde ha de ir a parar, descubriendo terreno según marcha, y cambiando de rumbo a medida que cambian las vistas que se abren a los ojos del espíritu. Esto es caminar sin plan previo.' This is equally true of the subjective reflections, generalizations, abstractions and opinions which alternate with the objective experiences — his thoughts on the hypocritical pretensions of the ant, of the man hurrying through the crowd, and of the *chocolatero*; his sympathy for the paralyzed beggar dragging himself along the ground; his wondering whether the acquaintance he greets is really of the same species as everyone else; his irritation with an automobile; and his renewed awareness of the inconvenience of having to carry his umbrella open.

The psychological realism of this passage is doubtless felt and intuitively accepted by most readers as an example of what in the Prologue to his *Tres novelas ejemplares* he called 'una realidad íntima, creativa y de voluntad' (II, 972), which in this case is the reality of an unpredictably free-flowing stream of conscious-ness. There is reason to believe also that Unamuno regarded this reality not only as a given truth concerning the human condition but as one to be actively promoted and maximized. In the essay *Adentro*, dated 1900, he rejected the idea of a 'plan previo', not in relation to literary creation but in life itself. Responding to a letter from a young friend, he writes: '¡Nada de plan previo, que no eres edificio! No hace el plan a la vida, sino que ésta lo traza viviendo... Tu vida es ante tu propia conciencia la revelación continua, en el tiempo, de tu eternidad, el desarrollo de tu símbolo, vas descubriéndote conforme obras' (I, 948).

Clearly, it is to a great extent in promotion of such an ideal of life itself that *Niebla* presents the kind of conception we find here of the life of Augusto Pérez, and advocates — and seems to exemplify — the mode of composition described by Víctor Goti. Paradoxically, the idea of living and writing 'sin plan previo' appears to be a basic 'plan previo' for this novel, giving rise to quite specific narrative techniques and modes of representation of subjective consciousness.

Having said that his novel's plot will simply develop out of itself, as the composition of his text progresses, Víctor immediately makes a similar statement about his characters: 'Mis personajes se irán haciendo según obren y hablen, sobre todo según hablen; su carácter se irá formando poco a poco. Y a las veces su carácter será el de no tenerlo', to which Augusto immediately adds, 'Sí, como el mío' (xvii, 615). Certainly the origins of such a conception of literary characters in the passage here quoted from *Adentro* are obvious enough, but Goti's literary ideas also develop and expand the essay's conception of human life. It is is quite literally true that literary characters have no reality other than that of the textual record of their acting and speaking — especially of their speaking —, it is also true that in accord with the view of real life found in *Adentro* one might say that the character of every human being is 'el de no tenerlo' — in the sense of never having definitive possession of any fixed character, any 'acabada personalidad...al principio de [su] vida.'[50]

[50] At a later point Víctor himself seems to insist that he and Augusto, like characters in a *nivola* (or perhaps he means because they are characters in a *nivola*) not only have no fixed character but no interiority whatever: 'Nosotros no tenemos dentro... El alma de un personaje de drama, de novela o de *nivola* no tiene más interior que el que le da... el lector' (xxx, 663). An error in the Austral edition (5), which has the reading 'no tiene más interior que el de la...', has led some critics to think he means the character of a *nivola* has no more interiority than his reader, and *vice versa*, although the feminine article is an obvious obstacle to such a reading.

When Augusto asks if in Víctor's novel there are psychology
and descriptions, his friend replies that what there is — rather
than either one, presumably — is dialogue, more than anything
else: 'La cosa es que los personajes hablen, que hablen mucho,
aunque no digan nada' (xvii, 615). Evidently Víctor believes that
this accords with the preferences of most readers: 'porque a la
gente le gusta la conversación por la conversación misma,
aunque no diga nada... Es el encanto de la conversación, de
hablar por hablar, del hablar roto e interrumpido' (xvii, 615-16).
Certainly this predominance of dialogue is very notable in
Niebla, and in all of Unamuno's novels following the first one.
One can, of course, say that there is also psychology in *Niebla*,
precisely because the characters reveal themselves through
speaking — to others or to themselves —, but explicit psychological commentary by the narrator is lacking, as is any explicit
description of setting.

In the Prologue to the 1923 edition of *Paz en la guerra*
Unamuno noted that in that early work there are 'pinturas de
paisaje y dibujo y colorido de tiempo y de lugar', but that in
subsequent work the novels are 'fuera de lugar y tiempo
determinados' (II, 91), while his taste for contemplating land-
scapes and evoking a sense of history is expressed in the many
essays recording his travels through Spain and Portugal. As
critics like Gullón have noted (*19*, p.95), the lack of explicit
descriptions does not prevent the reader from readily identifying
the setting of *Niebla* as that of a Spanish provincial capital in the
first quarter of the twentieth century, with its *paseos* —
occasionally interrupted by a few noisy automobiles —, its
casinos, its class distinctions, and its *chismografía*.

Continuing his comments on the creation of his novel's
characters through their speech, Víctor adds a very significant
requirement to his own method of characterization: 'Y sobre
todo que parezca que el autor no dice las cosas por sí, no nos
molesta con su personalidad, con su yo satánico' (xvii, 616). The
theme of the 'yo satánico', which in Unamuno's works goes
back at least as far as the essays of *En torno al casticismo*, seems
somewhat ironic in a thinker as concerned with his own *yo* as
Unamuno, but the recommended suppression of it is doubtless

the basis for the effect of an almost (though not completely) impersonal tone in the narrative portions of the text, and, more importantly, for the apparent autonomy of the literary characters. It is true that Víctor immediately adds that whatever his characters say is actually said by him, but Augusto, anticipating the position he will take in his conversation with Unamuno, says this is true only up to a certain point: 'Sí, que empezarás creyendo que los llevas tú, de la mano, y es fácil que acabes convenciéndote de que son ellos los que te llevan. Es muy frecuente que un autor acabe por ser juguete de sus ficciones...' (xvii, 616).

Víctor agrees this may be so but insists on his right — or in any case his intention — to include in his novel, however arbitrarily, whatever may occur to him, 'sea como fuere' (xvii, 616), which echoes the statement with which he introduced the subject of his novel — that is, that he intended to include in it, 'de cualquier manera', the story of don Eloíno. It is the repetition of this motif which — perhaps together with all the other unconventional aspects of the novel Víctor has described — prompts Augusto to remark: '—Pues acabará no siendo novela.' To this Víctor replies: 'No, será..., será... *nivola*' (xvii, 616). He then explains his invention of the term as suggested by the story of Manuel Machado's showing an unconventional sonnet to a critic whose only remark was, 'Pero ¡eso no es soneto!', to which the poet replied, 'No señor..., no es soneto, es... *sonite*' (xvii, 616). Both *sonite* and *nivola* suggest a certain general — perhaps superficial — resemblance to works bearing the traditional name of the genre by conserving the consonants of the familiar name, but the variation in its vocalic structure suggests a profound and substantial deviation from the established genre. It is also significant, of course, that the word *niebla* itself has the same consonantal structure as *novela* and *nivola*. When Víctor momentarily forgets the precise form of the word he has just invented and asks, '¿cómo dije?, *navilo...*, *nebulo*, no, no, *nivola*, eso es, ¡*nivola*!' (xvii, 616), we are given the sense that the *novela* is capable of undergoing a shifting series of transformations, as numerous and varied as the shapes assumed by a fog or mist. The transformational sequence *novela/navilo/*

nebulo/nivola/...niebla implies that *niebla* is the inevitable final stage of all such transformations, but at the same time it is the principle of the entire series. In the fullness of its possibilities for transformation the *novela* is equivalent to the *niebla*, in which the variety of potential forms is so close to infinite that they seem indistinguishable in one homogeneous, vaporous mass.

If in the fullest sense of the traditional genre *novela* ultimately is *niebla*, it is also true that *Niebla* is *novela*. This, at least, is what Unamuno suggests when in the 'Historia de *Niebla*' he says: 'Esta ocurrencia de llamarle *nivola*...fué otra ingenua zorrería para intrigar a los críticos. Novela y tan novela como otra cualquiera que así sea' ('Historia', 552). Later, in the prologue to *Tres novelas ejemplares*, he suggested that it is not merely as much a novel as any other but perhaps superlatively so: 'véase mi novela (¡y tan novela!) *Niebla*' (II, 971), which suggests that if the essence of the novel is *niebla*, *Niebla* is the essential novel. I do not mean to suggest we forget that in the transformational series *nivola* comes between *novela* and *Niebla*. Despite his later attempts to de-emphasize the difference between the *nivola* and the novel, it is clear that the former has its own characteristics, many of which I have at least indirectly already pointed out, both in this chapter and elsewhere, and I shall explicitly summarize them at the end of this chapter. It is also true that Víctor seems to recognize that in his novel he has created a new genre, and it is, in fact, largely for that reason that he has invented a new name for it: 'Así nadie tendrá derecho a decir que deroga las leyes de su género... Invento el género, e inventar un género no es más que darle un nombre nuevo, y le doy las leyes que me place' (xvii, 616).

Still, there is a basic ambiguity in Víctor's remarks, for to say that inventing a new genre is only a matter of giving it — that is, the old genre — a new name is to suggest that in itself his novel's genre is not necessarily new.[51] It is as if it were largely in order to spare himself the annoyance of being told that his work violated the 'leyes' or precepts of the novel, that he claimed he had

[51] Víctor's comments at this point seem to confirm what I have suggested in Chapter 1 concerning Unamuno's belief in the purely arbitrary and conventional nature of the linguistic sign, a doctrine formulated in modern linguistics by Ferdinand de Saussure. See Chapter 1, note 7.

created a new genre, with new 'leyes' which his work could not be said to violate, but this suggests he could just as easily have taken the position that the traditional 'leyes' of the novel are — or ought to be — quite flexible enough to permit him to call his work a novel. Yet having granted that he has, in fact, invented a new genre with new 'leyes', Víctor's final comment at this point is, '¡Y mucho diálogo!', making it clear that this is the first and greatest commandment in writing a *nivola*. When Augusto then asks what happens when a character is alone, Víctor replies: '—Entonces... un monólogo. Y para que parezca algo así como un diálogo invento un perro a quien el personaje se dirige' (xvii, 616).

At this point we realize that the 'personaje' of whom Víctor speaks is obviously Augusto Pérez, but much more is involved here than the simple irony of having a character of fiction writing another fiction (a fictional fiction) containing a character known to the (fictional) author in (fictional) real life. More significant than this, in fact, is the suggestion that the novel we are reading is the novel Víctor is writing. Víctor's *nivola* is *Niebla*, which at this point becomes totally self-reflexive. Even Augusto realizes that the effect is of his seeming to be in the process of being invented,[52] and the reader has the feeling of being in the process of reading a book in the process of being written, about a character in the process of being invented.

What, then, can be said by way of summary concerning the theory and practice of the *nivola*? First of all, it is characterized by a great predominance of talk, both dialogue and monologue,

[52] At this point there is a notable textual problem in many — perhaps all — editions of *Niebla*. The Escelicer edition (*4*), like the one in the first *Obras completas* (*2*), has Augusto saying: '¿Sabes, Víctor, que se me antoja que estás inventando?' (xvii, 616), which does not mean very much, since it is so obvious that Víctor is, indeed, inventing in a general sense. The text of the second *Obras completas* (*3*) has the same words exactly, but it removes the question marks and adds three periods as suspension points, as if the editors were aware that 'inventando' requires some direct object in order to be really meaningful. The first edition (*1*) and those of Brown (*7*) and Valdés (*8*) have: 'Sabes, Víctor, que se me antoja que me están inventando...', in which the third person plural can be regarded as equivalent to the passive voice, giving the meaning to which I allude in my comments above: 'You know, Víctor, I fancy I am being invented...'. In Stevens and Gullón (*6*), however, we find a reading which would give the passage its strongest meaning: '¿Sabes, Víctor, que se me antoja que me estás inventando?...', but unfortunately they include no justification for this departure from all previous editions.

through which the characters reveal their personalities and by which they are constituted. A corollary of this characteristic is the almost total absence of description of material setting and historical background. *Niebla* is not, of course, a pure dialogue novel, but the narrator's interventions serve principally to summarize events and attitudes of the characters. With respect to these characteristics there is no disparity between Goti's theory and Unamuno's practice of the *nivola*.

A second characteristic, closely related to the first, but in which there is some disparity between theory and practice, is the presence of characters who seem to have no fixed personality formed in advance of their entering into the action. This is true of Augusto Pérez, as it is for Unamuno's other *agonistas*, but most of the characters in *Niebla* are *antagonistas*, and many of them are caricatured embodiments of certain fixed attitudes and beliefs, as shown by Unamuno's frequent use of symbolic names, which even characterizes Augusto to some extent.

Another notable feature is a plot consisting of events which seem to move in simple succession, not linked by rigorous determinacy either of logic or of an apparent 'plan previo' of the author. A number of crucial events are presented as due to pure chance, as in the instance of Eugenia's passing Augusto's house just at the moment he goes out for a walk, or the accidental falling of a bird-cage, which makes it possible for him to gain entrance to her house. Analysis of structure and consideration of *Niebla*'s sources in Unamuno's previous writing and reading show that in practice it is not nearly as viviparous — that is, spontaneous and 'sin plan' — in its composition as Víctor's theory claims it to be, but even the indications one finds of careful structuring do not cancel the effect of free movement of the plot.

The *nivola* is also characterized by being highly meta-literary — concerned with its own literariness and with the nature of literature generally — as well as self-reflexive, tending to turn back on itself, becoming conscious of itself not only in its general literariness but in its specific textuality. When we realize that the text we are reading is presumably the text Víctor is writing, we feel the effect is virtually that of a telescoping of our familiar world of objective reality into a recognizable but purely mental world of linguistic, fictional, and intellectual reality. And *vice versa*, for when Augusto leaves his fictional provincial capital to visit the historical Miguel de Unamuno in the historical Salamanca, the opposite movement seems to occur. From this effect is derived what I see as a fifth distinguishing characteristic of the *nivola*, its apparent confusion of the planes of fiction and reality. When Augusto leaves Víctor he asks: 'Y esta mi vida, ¿es novela, es nivola o qué es? Todo esto que me pasa y que les pasa a los que me rodean, ¿es realidad o es ficción?' (xvii, 616), and there can be little doubt that the purpose is to raise the same question in the mind of the reader. In many other details, such as the uncertainty in which we are left as to whether it is Augusto or the author to whom the phrase, 'Se salió con la suya'[53] properly applies, the uncertainty of all efforts to know reality is constantly emphasized.

Some time after the conversation in which Víctor first spoke of his *nivola*, Augusto had a chance to read what had been written to that point, and his first comment — which the reader naturally associates with Augusto's own scenes with Rosario — is that 'ahí están cosas que rayan en lo pornográfico y hasta a las veces pasan de ello' (xxv, 647). Víctor insists, however, that they are mere 'crudezas', by which he means its frankness concerning the realities of physiological existence, particularly of human sexuality. None of these 'crudezas' is pornographic by our contemporary standards, certainly, but the frankness is a notable feature of the *nivola*.

It also is an important element in what I take to be the seventh and last of the principal characteristics of the type: the fact that it is profoundly humorous as well as profoundly serious. Its humour is that of the absurd, of disparity and contradiction, as in the contrast between the names Augusto and Pérez; between don Fermín's desire to promote understanding through Esperanto and his impeding understanding precisely by using it; between the protagonist's lofty idea of love and the egotism which so frequently besets it; and ultimately between the

[53] See the comments on the significance of the repetition of this phrase in the text of *Niebla* (xxxii, 674, 676) in Ribbans (*24*, p.138).

seriousness of its literary, psychological, existential, and meta-physical themes and the absurdity of its characters and situations.

What I say here of the *nivola* applies principally to *Niebla*, of course, but virtually all these characteristics are to be found in *Amor y pedagogía* and *Cómo se hace una novela* as well.[54] The *nivola* therefore stands as a well-defined and recognizable sub-genre, to be distinguished not so much from as within the novel, as a notable instance of the genre's manifold possibilities, which are as great as those of human thought and of language itself.

[54] Perhaps the most important respect in which *Cómo se hace una novela* differs from the other *nivolas* is in its almost purely tragic spirit, which is occasionally attenuated by moments of lyric sentiment but never by any humour. The 'crudezas' of physiological existence are, however, very much in evidence when Unamuno begins to speak of Spain's military directorate.

6. Conclusion: major themes

In the monologue which Augusto addresses to Orfeo following his first visit to the house of Eugenia, he comments on the significance of having taken a decisive step by finally entering her 'santuario' (vii, 577). Suddenly, however, his thoughts leap from the immediacy of this concrete fact to the broadest conceivable level of generality as he asks a series of highly metaphysical questions: '¡Un paso decisivo! Y dime, Orfeo, ¿qué necesidad hay de que haya ni Dios, ni mundo, ni nada? ¿Por qué ha de haber algo? ¿No te parece que esa idea de la necesidad no es sino la forma suprema que el azar toma en nuestra mente?' (vii, 577).

These questions are partly concerned with a problem of logic, particularly the logic of the concept of necessity, which presumably was prompted by doubt as to whether his 'paso decisivo' will necessarily have any particular results at all — that is, whether it really was decisive. At the same time, however, these are ontological questions, concerned with the problem as to why anything and everything exist at all. Two decades after the publication of *Niebla* Martin Heidegger asserted that the great question of metaphysics since the beginning of Western thought has always been some version of: 'Why are there any beings at all, rather than nothing?', a question he regards as eminently metaphysical because it inquires into the ground of all being, whether as source, foundation, or ultimate goal.[55]

Augusto's questions are clearly as cosmic in scope and as profound in their metaphysical depth as that formulated by Heidegger, and even if they do not explicitly include the 'rather

[55] Heidegger, *Introduction to Metaphysics*, trans. Ralph Manheim (New Haven: Yale University Press, 1959). The German original was published in 1953, but the lectures on which it is based were given in 1935. In any case, the work obviously had no influence whatever on *Niebla*, but I cite it because of the effectiveness with which it defines metaphysics in terms of the kind of questions it asks, as well as because of the striking similarity of Augusto's question to that of Heidegger.

than nothing', it is clear from *Niebla* as a whole that an awareness of nothingness as a constant alternative to being is never far
from the mind of Augusto Pérez or of Miguel de Unamuno. In
Chapter 3 I alluded to Augusto's metaphysical question as the
ultimate expression of his constant search for understanding —
for the resolution of an intellectual uncertainty which is the
transcendent projection of his own ontological insecurity, his
doubt as to how firmly grounded his own existence is in being.
Such an analysis is not meant to reduce the metaphysical themes
of *Niebla* to purely psychological themes, but to show how
thoroughly congruent the various thematic levels of the novel
ultimately are. Even the meta-literary dimension is inseparable
from the metaphysical and psychological dimensions of *Niebla*,
for to ask why and how and on what ground any existing thing
has being is to ask how and why and on what ground the
questioner himself and the products of his artistic imagination
have their being. It is no accident that the work I regard as the
ultimate *nivola* is entitled *Cómo se hace una novela*, which is
not, of course, a set of instructions showing how one does, in
fact, make a novel, but a meditation on the problem and the
mystery of how one brings into being upon the 'terrible
blancura' (VIII, 729) of a blank page the entity and entities
called a *novela*.[56] As he does so Unamuno makes it clear that he
is also contemplating the question of how a personality, a self, a
human consciousness, is brought into being and grounded in
being within the terrifying void or 'blancura' that surrounds it.

In *Niebla* the image and concept corresponding to that void of
non-being is *niebla* itself, but the same image — at the same time
— also symbolizes a plenitude of pure, indeterminate being,
since Unamuno regarded pure being and pure non-being as
identical.[57] It is this 'niebla tenebrosa', as it is called in the last

[56] The suggestion that *Cómo se hace una novela* is also a *nivola* is given support
in the extensive study of that work by Armando Zubizarreta, *Unamuno en su
'nivola'* (Madrid: Taurus, 1960).

[57] In his *Recuerdos de niñez y mocedad* (1908), Unamuno recalls the bewildering
impression made on him by learning from Balmes of Hegel's assertion of the
identity of pure being and pure nothingness. Later he came to know it directly
when he taught himself German by reading Hegel in the original. Unamuno's
library in Salamanca still has his copy of the *Logik*, from which he would have
learned that the identity is shown in the fact that pure being and pure nothingness are equally indeterminate concepts. One indication of the extent to which

occurrence of the word in the novel, from which all things come and to which they return. As Orfeo says of his master's dissolution in the mist of death, it is at the same time 'la niebla de que brotó y a que revertió' (Epílogo, 681). The pure-being/pure-nothingness of this 'niebla' is the ground of the existence of every determinate being, and the equivalent of that ontological ground in the realm of literature (although ultimately, of course, the literary is also subsumed in the ontological) is the pure, indeterminate potentiality of the novel, of which we become aware because *nivola* mediates the distance and the difference between *novela* and *niebla*. We therefore see again the complete congruence between the realm of the ontological and that of the literary in the themes of *Niebla*.

The tripartite symmetry of the implicit structure of this conception as to how things — real things or things of fiction — come to or fall from existence (*niebla*/existence/*niebla*) reminds us of the many other symmetries we have encountered, all of which are perhaps to some extent images of that fundamental structure of Unamuno's ontology. There is one important respect, however, in which *Niebla* teaches the lesson that such symmetries must be correctly understood as being realized within time, not in eternity. It would be quite natural, for example, to interpret Augusto Pérez's fantasy of the 'contra-historia' as implying a kind of constant and immediate eternal return in human life, with the simultaneous movement from 'fuente' to 'mar' and from 'mar' to 'fuente' (cf. Chapter 2 of this study), and a reversal of direction (he does not say whether on both levels) after death. When, however, he appears to Unamuno in a dream at the end of the novel, it is to tell him that his idea of reviving him in order to permit him to commit suicide if he wished is completely impossible: 'Sí, a un ente de ficción, como a uno de carne y hueso..., puede uno engendrarlo y lo puede matar, pero una vez que lo mató no puede, ¡no!, no puede resucitarlo' (xxxiii, 677). When Unamuno asks if he cannot

the paradox penetrated his thinking is the frequency with which he pointed out the fact that positive and negative concepts readily change into their polar opposites, as when *rem natum* changed from meaning something born — i.e., something which exists — to meaning *nada*. See, for example, '¡Res = Nada!' (VII, 1384-86) and '¡Plenitud de plenitudes y todo plenitud!' (I, 1171-82).

dream him again, he replies: 'No se sueña dos veces el mismo
sueño. Ese que usted vuelva a soñar y crea soy yo será otro'
(xxxiii, 678; cf. comments on this passage in Chapter 3 of this
study).[58] He thereby makes it clear that death has revealed to
him the reality of time, with its unidirectional movement from
present to future, and with this revelation has come an
awareness of the inauthentic conception of life which produced
the fantasy of the *contrahistoria* and Augusto's constant
unconscious desire to return to the mother. Linguistic creations
— even those as complex as novels — can be given symmetrical
structures which create an illusion of reversibility, or of being
turned back upon themselves in a timeless, objective autonomy,
but ultimately it must be recognized — and the life and death of
Augusto Pérez make this clear — that to live with this illusion is
the profoundest bad faith.

The illusions of language and the creations of language can in
other respects as well be seen as a fundamental theme of *Niebla*.
After Augusto's second encounter with Rosario he tells himself:
'La he estado mintiendo y he estado mintiéndome... El hombre
en cuanto habla miente, y en cuanto se habla a sí mismo, es
decir, en cuanto piensa sabiendo que piensa, se miente... La
palabra se hizo para exagerar nuestras sensaciones e impresiones
todas... acaso para creerlas... La única verdad es el hombre
fisiológico, el que no habla, el que no miente...' (xviii, 619).[59]
Much of this might at first be interpreted as mere cynicism
concerning the human propensity for lying, but I believe something much more radical is involved.

There is, in fact, good reason to believe that the contrast
between the realm of the physical (including the physiological)

---

[58] Unamuno did, in fact, revive Augusto Pérez to be an interlocutor in some of
his dialogue essays. See, for example, 'Una entrevista con Augusto Pérez' (VIII,
360-66).

[59] The meaning of 'acaso para creerlas' in this context is somewhat obscure.
Assuming it is equivalent to 'acaso para que las creamos', it perhaps means that
the word was invented so that we might believe in the reality of our own
emotions by giving them names. I strongly suspect, however, that the verb really
ought to be 'crearlas', since the idea that things are created by words is very
frequent in Unamuno, as when he has Víctor Goti say: 'En el principio fue la
Palabra y por la Palabra se hizo todo' (xxx, 663). Unfortunately, no justification
for this reading can be found in any of the editions, nor, so far as is known, in
the manuscript of *Niebla*.

and the realm of the verbal is to be understood in *Niebla* as constituting a profound dichotomy, as if into two entirely separate orders of reality, between which no real communication or exchange is possible. When Augusto says that the only truth is physiological man, I believe he means the only immediate truth, the truth which is that man. Any statement made about that man, however clear a conception it may give of the structures of that immediate truth, can never be that truth.

On the other hand, this radical dualism gives to language and the creations of language a kind of autonomy which frees it from subservience to that other reality, and may even make it superior to it. In Víctor's last conversation with Augusto his efforts to console his friend for the loss of Eugenia seem directed at trying to convince him that it all took place in a reality quite distinct from that of language and thought. Whatever loss and pain Augusto feels in that reality have no real effect on his mental and verbal reality. Augusto can still, as Víctor advises him, 'charlar, sutilizar, jugar con las palabras y los vocablos..., ¡pasar el rato!' (xxx, 663). Language is seen as the primary reality, because: 'En el principio fue la Palabra y por la Palabra se hizo todo' (xxx, 663). Despite the paraphrase of the Gospel of St John, this 'Palabra' is not to be identified with the transcendent Logos which is the Second Person of the Trinity, but with an impersonal Logos immanent in the realm of verbal reality, the faculty which generates specific utterances from the language system in which all possible utterances have potential form. Later Augusto and Víctor are discussing the famous maxim of Descartes, 'Pienso, luego soy' (xxx, 664), and Víctor denies that Descartes said it: 'Porque como Descartes no ha sido más que un ente ficticio, una invención de la historia, pues... ¡ni existió..., ni pensó!' (xxx, 664). When Augusto asks who, then, said it, Víctor replies: '—Eso no lo dijo nadie; eso se dijo ello mismo', from which Augusto concludes: '—Entonces, ¿el que era y pensaba era el pensamiento ése?', and Víctor answers: '—¡Claro! Y figúrate, eso equivale a decir que ser es pensar y lo que no piensa no es' (xxx, 664). To be is to think, and thought itself is being.

Víctor's approach to the mind-body problem is, therefore, to

attribute primary reality to the realm of mind, of thought, and
of language, but for Unamuno (and for Goti) the most basic
reality of that realm is unquestionably language.[60] To attribute
this ontological primacy to language and thought is what makes
it possible, in the first instance, to assert the autonomy — at
times even the primacy — of the creations of language, as when
Augusto tells Unamuno: 'Vamos a cuentas: ¿no ha sido usted el
que, no una, sino varias veces, ha dicho que Don Quijote y
Sancho son, no ya tan reales, sino más reales que Cervantes?'
(xxxi, 667). At the very least it seem clear that the belief in the
autonomy of language is the basis for every assertion of the
autonomy of works of literature, as well, of course, as literary
characters.

Occasionally, however, one encounters in the realm of
language and its literary creations evidence or at least
intimations of a longing for the other — the physical and pre-
linguistic — reality. The story of Augusto Pérez is that of a
linguistic entity which seeks to cross over from what Augusto in
his poem to Eugenia calls 'las brumas perdidas de la idea' (xxvii,
653) to the realm of the physical. In the fiction he claims to have
achieved it, telling her (in the same poem) that her eyes brought
his soul to bodily existence, but later it appears that this, too,
was a fiction and a fantasy, and that only the pain of being
abandoned permits him to say: '¡ahora sí, ahora me siento,
ahora me palpo, ahora no dudo de mi existencia real!' (xxx,
664). In the following chapter, however, Unamuno himself
reveals to the character and his reader that as an entity of fiction
Augusto Pérez is forever cut off from our familiar world of
palpable, physical reality. Despite all the paradoxes and wordplay which suggest the equivalence of the two realms — or even
the primacy of the linguistic one — the tragedy of Augusto
Pérez, like that of Don Quijote, reveals that the realm of
language and linguistic entities is always profoundly alienated
from the realm of the physical. Augusto Pérez, like his reader, is
a creature of language and thought, but the reader is so because

[60] In *Del sentimiento trágico de la vida* he expressed the idea that reason itself is
a product of language: 'Debe su origen acaso al lenguaje. Pensamos articulada,
o sea reflexivamente, gracias al lenguaje articulado, y este lenguaje brotó de la
necesidad de transmitir nuestro pensamiento a nuestros prójimos' (VII, 134).

he possesses language — a generative grammar open to the future and to ever new linguistic creations of his own. Augusto Pérez is a creature of language because he exists within and by it; he does not possess language but is possessed by it.

All of this may seem again to belabour the obvious, but the history of Western thought and Unamuno's own work gives abundant evidence that these are truths easily forgotten. The illusion of the ontological primacy of language is a snare which especially tempts the intellectual, the philosopher, and the man of letters. As Unamuno said in *Cómo se hace una novela*: 'Todos los que vivimos principalmente de la lectura y en la lectura, no podemos separar de los personajes poéticos o novelescos a los históricos... Todo es para nosotros libro, lectura... Somos bíblicos. Y podemos decir que en el principio fue el Libro' (VIII, 732). Outwardly the passage is as much an assertion of the primacy — for men of letters — of the linguistic and the literary as any of the statements made by the characters in *Niebla*. It is nevertheless not difficult to discern a nostalgia for palpable reality behind these words — a nostalgia as strong as Augusto's longing for it. The story of his failure is the novel's own deconstruction of the illusion upon which it is founded.

In conclusion, then, we can say that the major themes of *Niebla* are characterized both by their striking profundity and by the subtle indirection with which they are treated. To none of the metaphysical, psychological, literary, and linguistic questions which it raises does *Niebla* give answers, but it requires its readers to re-examine every traditional assumption concerning the nature of language, of the novel, of our own existence, and even the nature of Being itself.

Bibliographical Note

EDITIONS

1. *Niebla (Nivola)*, Prólogo de victor Goti (Madrid: Renacimiento, 1914). 2nd ed., 1928. 3rd ed., with an additional prologue titled 'Historia de *Niebla*' (Madrid: Espasa-Calpa, 1935). Of these the first edition is regarded as most authoritative. Now rare.
2. In *Obras completas*, II, pp.675–869, Introducción de M. Sanmiguel (Madrid: Afrodisio Aguado, 1951). This edition was begun in 1950, before some of Unamuno's major works were placed on the *Index*, and a warning was issued against dangers in other works.
3. Also in *Obras completas*, Nueva editión, II, pp.783–1000, ed. Manuel García Blanco (Barcelona: Vergara, Por concesión especial de Afrodisio Aguado, 1959). this edition and the previous one are easily confused since they have identical bindings and bear the name Afrodisio Aguado on the title page (the reference to Vergara appears on the back of that page and in the colophon). Some volumes in this edition are little more than reprintings of the earlier one, but certain texts are less reliable than before. *Niebla* does not seem to have suffered in this respect.
4. Also in *Obras completas*, II, pp.541–682, ed. Manuel García Blanco (Madrid: Escelicer, 1967). Now regarded as the standard edition. Much improved though not quite impeccable texts, including *Niebla*. This is the edition quoted here.
5. *Niebla (Nivola)*, Colección Austral, 99 (Buenos Aires:,Espasa-Calpe, 1939). Numerous reprintings since then in Buenos Aires and Madrid. Generally the most available popular edition, but it contains some deceptive errors not found in other editions.
6. *Niebla (Nivola)*, Introducción de Harriet Stevens y Ricardo Gullón (Madrid: Taurus, 1965, reprinted 1977). Another popular edition. Excellent introduction.
7. *Niebla (Nivola)*, ed. Penny Brown (London: Harrap, 1976). An excellent school edition, with introduction, notes, and vocabulary. Reprints text of 1914 edition.
8. *Niebla*, ed. Mario J. Valdés (Madrid: Cátedra, 1982). Critical edition, based on those published in Unamuno's lifetime, as well as on a

manuscript dated 1907. Editor's 'Comentario' analyses what he identifies as five successive and cumulative stages of textual reality presented in the novel. Useful information on history of the text.

ENGLISH TRANSLATIONS

9. *Mist: A Tragicomic Novel*, trans. Warner Fite (New York: Knopf, 1928, reprinted 1973). Long the only translation.
10. *Mist*, trans. Anthony Kerrigan, in *Selected Works of Miguel de Unamuno*, VI, Bollingen Series, 85 (Princeton: University Press, 1976). also in British edition (London: Routledge and Kegan Paul, 1976). Interesting introduction by translator and Foreword by Jean Cassou. Useful notes by Martin Nozick and translator.

BIOGRAPHIES

11. Margaret R. Rudd, *The Lone Heretic: A Biography of Miguel de Unamuno y Jugo* (Austin: University of Texas Press, 1963). The only biography in English. Occasionally excessively speculative.
12. Emilio Salcedo, *Vida de Don Miguel*, 2a ed. (Salamanca: Anaya, 1970). By far the most extensive biography available.

GENERAL STUDIES

13. Robert Alter, *Partial Magic: The Novel as a Self-Conscious Genre* (Berkeley: University of California Press, 1975). Study of the self-conscious novel, from Cervantes to Claude Mauriac. The pages on *Niebla* are relatively few and not fully accurate as summary. Highly useful, nevertheless, for the presentation of Unamuno's novel in historical and comparative perspective.
14. Ana María Barrenechea, 'Unamuno en el movimiento de renovación de la novela europea'. In *Collected Studies in Honour of Américo Castro's Eightieth Year* (Oxford: Lincombe Lodge Research Library, 1965), pp.39–47. A brief but important discussion of Unamuno's innovations in the representation of character, setting, and plot.
15. R.E. Batchelor, *Unamuno Novelist: A European Perspective* (Oxford: Dolphin, 1972). Mainly concerned with parallels between Unamuno and other leading European writers, most of whom are his predecessors or contemporaries, but including some, like Sartre and Camus, whose work is more recent. Sometimes unconvincing, but interesting in suggesting a broader conceptual context within which Unamuno may be read.

Niebla

16. Carlos Blanco Aguinaga, *El Unamuno contemplativo* (México: El
    Colegio de México, 1959; 2nd ed., Barcelona: Laia, 1975). May well
    be the single most important study of Unamuno to date. Contrasts the
    contemplative Unamuno, willing to lose himself in cosmic and
    spiritual totalities, with the agonistic, self-affirming and
    individualistic Unamuno who attracted the greater public attention.
    Important for the study of *Niebla* in showing how the memory of
    Augusto's dead mother becomes a misty presence pervading the entire
    novel.
17. Carlos Feal Deibe, *Unamuno, 'El Otro' y Don Juan* (Madrid: Cupsa,
    1976). The most explicitly psychoanalytic study of Unamuno to date.
    Highly interesting chapter on *Niebla*, most of which is entirely
    convincing.
18. José Ferrater Mora, *Unamuno: Philosophy of Tragedy* (Berkeley:
    University of California Press, 1962). Translation of *Unamuno:
    bosquejo de una filosofi* (Buenos Aires: Sudamericana, 1957). An
    excellent general study, with emphasis on philosophical aspects of the
    work.
19. Ricardo Gullón, *Autobiografías de Unamuno* (Madrid: Gredos, 1964).
    Emphasizes, as the title suggests, the concept of authorial presence
    and self-revelation in Unamuno's texts. Excellent in studies both of
    broad themes and of individual works.
20. Paul Ilie, *Unamuno: An Existential View of Self and Society*
    (Madison: University of Wisconsin Press, 1957). Interesting
    discussion of problems of personality and existence in the thought of
    Unamuno, with particular reference to parallels in that of Nietzsche.
21. Juan López-Morillas, 'Unamuno y sus criaturas: Antolín S. Paparrigó-
    pulos', *Cuadernos Americanos*, 7 (1948), 234–49. Reprinted in
    Intelectuales y espirituales (Madrid: Revista de Occidente, 1961).
    Important not only for its discussion of Paparrigópulos but also for the
    typology it offers of Unamuno's literary characters generally.
22. Julián Marías, *Miguel de Unamuno* (Madrid: Espasa-Calpe, 1942).
    One of the earliest and still one of the best general studies of
    Unamuno's thought, which Marías has recognized as most
    authentically represented in the novels. This study is centred on what
    Unamuno in *Del sentimiento trágico* called the 'única cuestión' of the
    destiny of human consciousness after death.
23. Antonio Regaldo García, *El siervo y el señor* (Madrid: Gredos, 1968).
    A study stressing the nineteenth-century origins of Unamuno's
    thought. Sometimes a little arbitrary but interesting.
24. Geoffrey Ribbans, *Niebla y soledad* (Madrid: Gredos, 1971).
    Particularly significant are Chapter III, 'La evolución de la novelística
    unamuniana: *Amor y pedagogía y Niebla*, previously published in

English in *Hispanic Studies in Honour of I. González Llubera*, ed.
Frank Pierce (Oxford: Dolphin, 1959), pp.269–85, and Chapter IV,
'Estructura y significado de *Niebla*', an earlier version of which
appeared in the *Revista de la Universidad de Madrid*, 13 (1965),
211–40. A briefer essay on the same theme, 'The Structure of
Unamuno's *Niebla*', appears in *Spanish Thought and Letters in the
Twentieth Century*, ed. Germán Bleiberg and Inman Fox (Nashville:
Vanderbilt University Press, 1966), pp.395–406.

25. Antonio Sánchez Barbudo, *Estudios sobre Galdós, Unamuno y
Machado* (Madrid: Gredos, 1968). Recent edition of essays on
Unamuno's religious thought. Much debated for their thesis of an
atheistic and hypocritical Unamuno, but of basic importance.

26. David G. Turner, *Unamuno's Webs of Fatality* (London: Tamesis,
1974). Substantial and scholarly study of the theme of destiny in the
novels. particularly interesting comments on interweaving of concepts
and images to form narrative structures.

27. Frances Wyers, *Miguel de Unamuno: The Contrary Self* (London:
Tamesis, 1976). An interesting study of Unamuno's thought on the
problem of human personality and the themes of the divided self, the
double and the dream.

ESSAYS ON 'NIEBLA'

28. Carlos Blanco Aguinaga, 'Unamuno's *Niebla*: Existence and the Game
of Fiction', *MLN*, 79 (1964), 188–205. Excellent study of the
existential problem represented by Augusto Pérez, and the
significance of his dialogue with the author.

29. Leon Livingstone, 'The Novel as Self-Creation', in José Rubia Barcia
and M.A. Zeitlin, *Unamuno: Creator and Creation* (Berkeley:
University of California Press, 1967), pp.92–115. Discusses
Unamuno's thought on creation of the self through literary creation. A
general thematic study, but largely about *Niebla*.

30. Ciriaco Morón-Arroyo, '*Niebla* en la evolución temática de
Unamuno', *MLN*, 81 (1966), 143–58. Rigorous analysis of *Niebla* as
representing a crucial stage in Unamuno's thought on the problem of
personality.

31. Paul R Olson, 'Unamuno's *Niebla*: The Question of the Novel',
Georgia Review, 29 (1975), 652–72. An essay from which parts of the
present study have been developed.

32. Alexander A. Parker, 'On the Interpretation of *Niebla*'. In Barcia and
Zeitlin (see *29*), pp.116–38. Particularly good on the contrasts
between innocence and knowledge, the physiological and the
intellectual, and language and truth. One of the first studies to make

clear the importance of the erotic in *Niebla*. A Spanish version appears in *Miguel de Unamuno*, ed. Antonio Sánchez Barbudo (Madrid: Taurus, 1974).

33. Harriet S. Stevens, 'Las novelitas intercaladas en *Niebla*. *Insula*, no.170 (Jan. 1961), 1. Studies interpolated tales in relation to themes of the principal narrative and shows that they enhance conceptual unity in spite of interrupting narrative.

34. Ruth House Webber, 'Kierkegaard and the Elaboration of Unamuno's *Niebla*', *Hispanic Review*, 32 (1964), 118–34. Shows numerous possible influences from *Either/Or* and *Concluding Unscientific Postscript*, as well as valuable insights into the significance of Unamuno's use of those models.

35. Frances Weber, 'Unamuno's *Niebla*: From Novel to Dream', *PMLA*, 88 (1973), 209–18. a highly interesting study of psychological and existential aspects of Unamuno's thought on dreams and other psychological and existential themes. This essay is the basis for the author's treatment of *Niebla* in her general study of Unamuno (*27*), where she signs herself Frances Wyers.

SUPPLEMENTARY BIBLIOGRAPHY

EDITIONS

36. Cifo González, Manuel. Colección Arbolí, 24 (Tarragona: Tarraco, 1986). Readily accessible classroom edition based on that of 1935 (see *1*). Introduction differs from this Guide in describing structure simply as a sequence of six *núcleos*, *bloques*, or *episodios*, and in counting six interpolated tales, among which the story of Víctor Goti is said to have four parts. Brief bibliography and suggested student exercises.

37. Germán Gullón, Colección Austral, 115 (Madrid: Espasa-Calpe, 1990). Supersedes *5* as the 23rd printing of the novel in this series, but with a thoroughly revised text, based on first edition (*1*). Excellent introductory essay. Helpful notes, good bibliography.

38. Isabel Paraíso, Biblioteca Crítica de Autores Españoles, 44 (Barcelona: Plaza & Janés, 1985). A useful student edition based on that of 1935 (see *1*), with introduction discussing author's life and works, and *Niebla*'s sources, themes, and structure. Recognizes structural symmetry only in the balancing of the two prologues and two epilogues. Unique in counting only three interpolated tales (contrast *36*). Also contains brief bibliography and list of topics for student essays.

GENERAL STUDIES

39. Roberta Johnson, *Crossfire: Philosophy and the Novel in Spain,
    1900–1934* (Lexington: Univ. Press of Kentucky, 1993). Excellent
    study of early-twentieth-century Spanish novel in relation to European
    intellectual history. Devotes a chapter each to *Amor y pedagogía* and
    Niebla, interpreting them as attacks on positivism, idealism, and
    ultimately on European rationalism in general.
40. Gayana Jurkevich, *The Elusive Self: Archetypal Approaches to the
    Novels of Miguel de Unamuno* (Columbia: Univ. of Missouri Press,
    1991). Studies both the novels and the personality of Unamuno in
    terms of C.G. Jung's analytical psychology, interpreting protagonists'
    struggles as efforts of the individual consciousness to liberate itself
    from the maternal archetype. See especially Chapter 3, '*Niebla*: A
    Struggle for Individuation'.
41. Thomas Mermall, 'The Chiasmus: Unamuno's Master Trope', *PMLA*,
    105 (1990), 245–55. Excellent study of conceptual implications in
    Unamuno's use of the syntactic and rhetorical figure called chiasmus.
    Implicitly confirms this Guide's analysis of the chiastic structure of
    Niebla.
42. Gonzalo Navajas, *Miguel de Unamuno: bipolaridad y síntesis
    ficcional: una lectura posmoderna* (Barcelona: PPU, 1988). Studies
    Unamuno in terms of the poststructuralist and postmodernist thought
    of Jacques Derrida, Paul de Man, and others. Sees Unamuno's
    variously interpreted dualism as opposition between dualism itself, as
    expressed in essays, and unitary synthesis in works of fiction. Believes
    that understanding Unamuno is also an aid to understanding
    postmodernist theory.
43. Paul R. Olson, 'Sobre las estructuras quiásticas en el pensamiento
    unamuniano (interpretación de un juego de palabras)', in *Homenaje a
    Juan López-Morillas*, ed. José Amor y Vázquez & A. David Kossoff
    (Madrid: Castalia, 1982), pp.359–68. A general study of Unamuno's
    use of chiasmus is the point of departure for analysis of chiastic
    strucuture in *Niebla*.
44. ——. 'Unamuno and the Primacy of Language: Trajectory of a Critical
    Tradition', in *Studies in Honor of Bruce W. Wardropper*, ed. Dian Fox
    et al. (Newark, DE: Juan de la Cuesta Hispanic Monographs, 1989),
    pp.205–19. Survey of studies on Unamuno's theories of language,
    from Wardropper to Alan Lacy and others. Concludes that for
    Unamuno himself the true primacy is that of material reality.
45. Geoffrey Ribbans, 'Dialéctica de lucha y ambigüedad en la novelística
    unamuniana', in *Actas del Congreso Internacional Cincuentenario de*

Unamuno (Salamanca: Univ., 1989), pp.153–64. Returns to the
critic's survey (see *24*) of the evolution of Unamuno's novels, with
further discussion of questions concerning unresolved conflict and
ambiguity. Recognizes possibilities for multiple interpretations of the
novels, but regards conflict and ambiguity themselves as fundamental
to their meaning. Believes, for example, that in *Niebla* the cause of
Augusto's death is therefore deliberately left undecided. Contains
many new insights into questions addressed in *24*, as well as into
other aspects of the novels.

46.   Iris Zavala, *Unamuno y el pensamiento dialógico* (Barcelona:
      Anthropos, 1991). Seeks to identify in Unamuno an example of the
      dialogic thinking which Mikhail Bakhtin has analysed in the work of
      Dostoevski. Sees this tendency in Unamuno as a mark of modernity,
      postmodernity, and poststructuralism *avant la lettre* (cf. *43* and see
      59).

ESSAYS ON 'NIEBLA'

47.   Rosendo Díaz-Peterson, 'Sobre el dinamismo científico de *Niebla*', in
      Volumen-homenaje a Miguel de Unamuno (Salamanca: Univ., 1986)
      [hereafter *VHMU*], pp.383–93. Discusses Unamuno's concept of
      scientific thought as essentially static, in contrast to the dynamism of
      life. Sees *Niebla* as structured by successive manifestations of this
      contrast, and as moving toward a scientific dynamism. Marred to a
      certain extent by misunderstanding of some previous criticism.

48.   Arturo A. Fox, 'El Edipo en Unamuno: el caso de *Niebla*', in *Selected
      Proceedings of the Singularidad y Trascendencia Conference*
      (Boulder:SSSAS, 1990), pp.99–105. Interesting and largely convincing
      study of Augusto Pérez in psychoanalytic terms. Explicitly based on
      Jacques Lacan's theory of mental life as a world of symbols structured
      like language.

49.   Germán Gullón, 'Reinterpretación de *Niebla*: el carácter de la
      comunicación literaria', *Nueva Revista de Filología Hispánica*, 35
      (1987), 293–98. Applies speech-act theory to the study of *Niebla*
      through analysis of the interpolated tale of the *fogueteiro*, showing
      how that tale, and the whole novel, have turned from the 'constative
      speech' characteristic of realism to the self-referential and self-
      effecting 'performative speech' characteristic of the modern novel.
      Partly anticipates introductory essay in *37*.

50.   Roberta Johnson, 'El problema del conocimiento en Unamuno y la
      composición de *Niebla*', in *Actas del IX Congreso Internacional de
      Hispanistas*, ed. Sebastian Neumeister (Frankfurt-am-Main: Vervuert,
      1989), II, pp.303–08. Studies *Niebla*'s theme of contrast between the

intellectual, the sensorial, and the physiological, relating it to theories of Ramón Turró, who traced the development of human knowledge and self-knowledge to the biological drive to satisfy hunger.

51. ———. 'Hunger and Desire: The Origins of Knowledge in *Niebla*', in *Selected Proceedings* (see *48*), pp.93–98. Later version of *50*, clarified and made more explicit in a number of ways.

52. Gayana Jurkevich, 'Unamuno's Anecdotal Digressions: Practical Joking and Narrative Structure in *Niebla*', *Revista Hispánica Moderna*, 45 (1992), 5–13. Independently confirms some aspects of this Guide's original analysis of the interpolated tales, both with respect to the number of those properly regarded as interpolations, and in terms of their structural function. Also contains interesting and original observations on other aspects of the tales.

53. Paul R. Olson, 'Sobre las estructuras de *Niebla*', *VHMU*, pp.423–34. Further analysis of chiastic structure in *Niebla*, distinguishing that of the novel's *historia* (the life of Augusto Pérez) from the structure of its *discurso narrativo* (the textual form in which his life is presented).

54. Nelson R. Orringer, '*Niebla* y Dios:una desconocida fuente teológica', *VHMU*, pp.435–56. Finds in Unamuno's personally annotated copy of a book by George Wobbermin on theology and metaphysics (1901) a probable source for the analogy drawn in *Niebla* between the relation of author to character and that of God to man.

55. Pilar Palomo, 'La estructura orgánica de *Niebla*: nueva aproximación', *VHMU*, pp.457–73. Independently confirms this Guide's analysis of structural function of interpolated tales, although mistakenly reversing order of the first two. Extends concept of symmetry to uses of term *niebla* as metaphysical symbol (first five and last five chapters) and to measured time (first and last four) against unmeasured or indeterminate time.

56. Janet Pérez, 'Rhetorical Integration in Unamuno's *Niebla*', *Revista Canadiense de Estudios Hispánicos*, 8 (1983–84), 49–73. A useful and very thorough inventory of repeated motifs, images, and themes (e.g. *niebla, sueño, azar*, chess, eyes, stars, women's hands, birds, triads, relations between the sexes, fiction vs reality), all presented for the purpose of demonstrating that *Niebla* could not have been composed 'sin plan previo', as Víctor's formula for the *nivola* would presumably have required. Less convincing is the critic's conclusion that the entire concept of the *nivola* can therefore not be taken seriously.

57. Emma Sepúlveda, 'Reducción y expansión: las novelas intercaladas en *Niebla*', *Crítica Hispánica*, 7 (1985), 133–40. Discusses ways in which the interpolated tales present in condensed form many of the events and themes of the novel itself, as well as expanding our view of

the various facets of the protagonist's personality and of the range of possible courses of action lying before him.

58. Robert C. Spires, 'From Augusto Pérez to Alejandro Gómez to Us', *Revista de Estudios Hispánicos* (USA), 20 (1986), 39–49. Although commenting more extensively on 'Nada menos que todo un hombre' than on *Niebla*, this essay is an interesting study of Augusto Pérez as an essential link in the evolution of Unamuno's conception of the autonomous character in fiction and of the ontological uncertainty of the human condition.

59. Iris Zavala, '*Niebla*: la lógica del sueño', *La Torre*, n.s., 1 (1987), 69–92. An earlier version of Chapter III in *46*. Analysis centred on the interview between Augusto and his author in *Niebla*, xxxi, intended to show how basic in Unamuno's thought is something author calls 'diálogo infinito' or 'contradicción permanente', forming unity without synthesis of polar opposites: birth/death, affirmation/negation, reality/fiction, tragedy/comedy.

CRITICAL GUIDES TO SPANISH TEXTS

Edited by
J.E. Varey, A.D. Deyermond & C. Davies

CRITICAL GUIDES TO SPANISH TEXTS

Edited by
J.E. Varey, A.D. Deyermond & C. Davies